CANADA
AND THE
WORLD

CANADA
AND THE
WORLD

Agenda for the
Last Decade
of the Millennium

Anatol Rapoport
Anthony Rapoport

Science for Peace
Samuel Stevens & Co.
Toronto 1992

Science for Peace
University College
University of Toronto

Samuel Stevens & Co.
University of Toronto Press
5201 Dufferin Street
Downsview, Ontario M3H 5T8
Canada

Canadian Cataloguing in Publication Data

Rapoport, Anatol
    Canada and the World

Includes bibliographic references and index.
ISBN 0-88866-636-5

1. Canada — Relations. 2. Canada — Military policy.
3. World politics — 1989- . 4. Peace.
5. International Cooperation. I. Rapoport, Anthony,
1962- . II. Science for Peace (Association). III. Title.

FC602.R36 1992   327.71   C92-093011-5
F1034.2.R36 1992

Cover: Blackbird Design

Printed on paper
containing over 50%
recycled paper including
10% post-consumer fibre.

CONTENTS

V.   RELATIONS WITH THE UNITED STATES

VI   RELATIONS WITH THE THIRD WORLD

VII.   CANADA'S POSITION IN A NEW WORLD ORDER

VIII. IMPLICATIONS FOR DOMESTIC POLICY

PREFACE

This book is the product of a collective effort by some members of the Group of 78. The name of the group derives from the number of its founding members. Its activities comprise studies of and analysis of public issues which seem at the time to be of crucial importance not only to Canadians but to all the inhabitants of the planet. The issues are discussed at annual conferences and some of the discussions have been edited and published.

The present effort was stimulated by the rapid changes in the political landscape of Eastern Europe and the consequent demise of the Cold War. It seemed at the time that those changes were about to usher in a new historical era, rich in unprecedented opportunities of improving human life, in particular of freeing humanity from the threats generated by the burgeoning arsenals of weapons of total destruction and by the degradation of the environment. It seemed that global collective effort directed at solving urgent global problems became suddenly possible. One could speak hopefully of an "agenda" for such collective effort.

On August 2, 1990, the whole outlook suddenly changed. What was feared – an explosion of violence in the Middle East – suddenly became stark reality. In a few months a major war erupted, and all talk about a "peace dividend" and of a major victory of the forces of peace suddenly appeared to be no more than wishful fantasies. One could almost hear the derisive laughter of the "realists."

By that time, the bulk of this book was already written. Against the background of unfolding disaster, it seemed pitifully out of date. But almost everything one could write about the current world situation would almost surely become out of date before it could be published. To rewrite the book appeared futile. On the other hand, nothing that we wrote lost any of its pertinence. On the contrary, if we were to "bring the book up to date," we would only add to it and would, in fact, welcome the opportunity to relate what we already wrote to what has been happening. The formidable problems mentioned in this taking stock of the state of the world will still be with us long after the war in the Gulf is over and regardless of its outcome. To be sure, they will become more difficult, and Canada's role in contributing to the solution of these problems will also become more difficult, because Canada's reputation as peace keeper has been tarnished by Canada's unnecessary and futile participation in this war. However, there is no choice but to continue to exert efforts if only to set an example to our children, who may have to go on with the struggle. As someone rightly pointed out, we did not inherit this home in space from our parents; we borrowed it from our children. Decency demands that we return it to them in a decent condition.

Acknowledgements

The following members of the Group of 78 and friends sympathetic to its aims contributed to this work by submitting copy, directing us to sources, making cogent suggestions for substantive revisions or stylistic improvements:

Newton R. Bowles
Soonoo Engineer
Shirley Farlinger
Ann Gertler
Leonard Johnson
Peter Meincke
Gwen Rapoport
Ronald Shirtliff
Anne Williams
Pat Woodcock

Two of us undertook collating the submitted copy, writing our own contributions, and editing cumulated material. To all who helped we render our heartfelt thanks. Needless to say, any shortcomings or errors are to be debited only to us.

> Anatol Rapoport
> Anthony Rapoport
> Toronto, March 15, 1991

I. A NEW PHASE OF HISTORY

A Changed World

In the last decade of this century the world will be very different from the world we have known. We are concerned with Canada's position in this new world. The catalytic agent for the radical change we have witnessed was the Revolution of 1989. The revolution was a genuine one: it changed the fundamental character of the regimes of Eastern Europe and of the Soviet Union.

This change seems to have ended the superpower confrontation which has dominated world politics since the end of World War II. Historically, power rivalries have generally ended in wars and in realignments of military alliances, substituting new power struggles for old ones. The present change appears different. It has occurred in a way that seems to open opportunities for global cooperation, for jointly attacking problems of concern to the entire population of this planet.

When this book was started, it seemed that the principal obstacle to grasping these opportunities, namely, the institutionalized enmity between the United States and the Soviet Union, had been swept away. By the time the first draft was finished, however, a shift of attention toward global problems again seemed remote. A major war broke out in the Middle East with consequences impossible to foresee. Possibly we are entering a transitional period so turbulent that any discussion of an "agenda" for even the immediate future is futile. We will, nevertheless, assume that whatever be the outcome of the present crisis, the end of the Cold War formalized by the non-aggression pact between NATO and Warsaw Pact countries was a decisive event of our time. We will assume that henceforth world politics will be no longer dominated by the rivalry of the great powers.

If our assumption is justified, the role of middle powers can become most important. By middle powers we mean those that have not acquired vast destructive potential but carry considerable economic weight. They have a sufficiently high profile to exert an influence in world affairs. Canada is a prime example of such a power. We feel that Canada can provide leadership in setting a new global agenda.

The new role of the middle powers can be seen in the perspective of the new phase in the history of the Western world. Two precedents of such "changes of phase" come to mind: the Renaissance in 15th century Europe and the Enlightenment in 18th century France.

The Renaissance took about two centuries to blossom. It ushered in a new phase of human history by pushing to the forefront of human consciousness the autonomy of the human individual. It culminated in the Reformation. In the 18th century, the Age of Enlightenment ushered in reason as a major mode of thought and paved the way for the crucial role of science in human affairs by dismantling dogma and superstition in the realm of natural phenomena. The Enlightenment culminated in the French Revolution. It pushed the notion of equality of human beings to the forefront of human consciousness.

Historical change now moves faster. The ideational preparation for the East European Revolution of 1989 took less than a half century.

To see the connection between the present change and the two previous ones, consider the concerns that suddenly lost their relevance in each case. The Renaissance marked a shift of focus from concerns with the Other World to keen interest (and delight) in the world of the senses. The autonomy of the individual, emphasised in the ideology of the Reformation, was the formal recognition of this shift. The Enlightenment marked the rejection of ideas inherent in absolute monarchy and a divinely prescribed social order. The French Revolution and the attendant sprouting of democratic ideals were consequences. The present new phase of European history may be marked by the blossoming of global concerns and the consequent eclipse of concerns revolving around the struggle for power.

Ever since the Americas were settled by Europeans, Canada's policies have been based in large measure on strategic connections to European politics. One can reasonably expect a transformation in response to the transformation of Europe.

One can place the beginning of the new phase about 1985, when the Soviet Union opted out of its confrontational posture. Clearly, this does not mean that its capacity to destroy civilization was suddenly dissipated. The missiles and the warheads are still there. So are the tanks and the planes. And even if drastic cuts are made in the nuclear and/or conventional arsenals, there will still be enough left to destroy civilization. But the readiness of the Soviet Union to fight a war has practically vanished.

The sceptic will point out that the rhetoric should not be taken at face value, that "peace offensives" have been periodically launched by Soviet leaders without in the least reflecting any credible abandonment of the threat posture or of the determination to retain their grip on an empire and, perhaps, to expand it when opportunities arose. Our conjecture that the present "peace offensive" differs fundamentally from previous ones is based on the evidence that not only has the ideological framework of Soviet Communism deteriorated but the bankruptcy of the ideology has been fully recognized and admitted by the present leadership of the Soviet Union. Moreover, this recognition and admission have resulted in cataclysmic political changes which have deprived the concept of the "Soviet threat" (as well as that of the Soviet Empire) of any meaning.

If "Soviet threat" is to be more than a compulsive repetition of three syllables, it behooves those who invoke the image to indicate concretely who or what is threatened by what means and what is to be accomplished by carrying out the threatened actions.

Traditionally the "Soviet threat" has been depicted in two scenarios. One posited a sudden nuclear attack on the U.S.; the other an invasion of Western Europe with the view of incorporating it into the "Soviet empire." The first scenario was dictated by the Pearl Harbor syndrome, a consequence of the dominance of recent historical experience over military leaders' perception of their tasks. This syndrome has now practically faded. If a Pearl Harbor-type attack still figures in some Pentagon scenarios, it does so on purely formal grounds in the context of what amounts to textbook exercises.

Whether or not there has ever been a threat of a Soviet invasion of Western Europe, there can be no such threat now. For a threat to exist, there must be some evidence of readiness and capability to carry it out. In the present political climate of Eastern Europe and, indeed, in the Soviet Union there is neither readiness nor capability. The preparation of a massive invasion involves planning of enormous, precisely coordinated military actions, solutions of formidable logistic problems, reinforcing the armed forces and mobilization of populations, including those of the allies, which have now without exception opted out of any such undertaking if, indeed, they had ever been willing to participate in it. We need only compare the present situation with that in Europe of the 1930s, when Hitler's war plans were highly visible and, at least initially, entirely realistic, to appreciate the absurdity of attributing such plans to the Soviet Union and to its erstwhile allies.

It is this sudden removal of all basis of belief in the "Soviet threat," on which the Cold War thrived, that created the opportunity to shift the focus of attention from the struggle for power to truly global problems that can be solved by global thinking and renunciation of the we-they dichotomy where it fixates enmities based on nation, ideology, race, or class.

What is more remarkable is that such a shift of focus from parochial to global thinking (which became the stimulus of the East European Revolution) was formally announced by the leader of a state in which, ever since its foundation, an ideology based on a dogma of irreconcilable struggle (the "class struggle") has played the part of a state religion.

The Paramount Issues

Once we turn our attention from parochial to global concerns, we recognize three terminal threats. These are:

The threat of demise by activation of weapons of total destruction — This threat is to civilization, quite possibly to humanity. Until recently, this has been the most immediate, the most widely publicized, and the most vividly imagined threat – the prospect of an "end with a bang." It has been attenuated, but it has not disappeared.

The threat of demise through despoliation and degradation of the planet — Awareness of this threat in the general public has grown steadily since the early 1970s. Evidence of its reality has grown dramatically in the last decades. This sort of demise, an "end with a whimper," would be as complete as the "end with a bang."

The threat of perpetual endemic violence — Conflicts originating in the tremendous disparities between the comfortable and the destitute are fueled by ruthless exploitation of the powerless. Sooner or later these conflicts will engulf the affluent world: conflicts over scarce resources; terrorism developed into a new kind of warfare involving sophisticated "high tech." by means of which the weak can wreak destruction on the strong. No one is safe from this violence.

Each of these threats could be lethal, but the degree of immediacy differs. Probably the threat of nuclear annihilation is the most immediate. The "end with a bang" could be a matter of a few years or a few months. The threat of degradation of the environment to the point when it can no longer support human life is, perhaps, less immediate, but the denouement, if no countermeasures are taken, is more certain than a nuclear holocaust. The period of grace is, perhaps, some decades. The increase in the level of chronic global violence is already apparent, though it still resembles a smouldering fire. When it will burst into a furious conflagration is not known, but its effect – the erosion and final destruction of civilization – is practically certain. The removal of this threat – the threat of chronic violence spread throughout the entire planet – requires the integration of the impoverished world into a global community. This can be done only if a cooperative human community comes into being – a precondition for the removal of the other two threats.

II. THE THREAT OF AN END WITH A BANG

Since the foreign policy of Canada has become strongly associated with that of the United States, a discussion of Canadian policies in the context of an agenda for the nineties must be coupled with an analysis and evaluation of American policies.

What Has Changed and What Hasn't

Writing in the midst of rapid development, we must face the possibility that conditions described as persistent may be changed by the time this is published. We can, however, record both the changes and the persistencies observed so far. In these we can perceive tendencies which may continue.

Since the demise of the doctrinaire and dictatorial regimes in the Soviet Union and in Eastern Europe, the fear on the part of the West of instant annihilation by weapons of total destruction has been attenuated. After the agreement of the Big Two to remove medium range missiles from Europe, the clock on the cover of the *Bulletin of Atomic Scientists* (which indicates minutes to the "end with a bang") was moved back from 11:57 to 11:54. After the sweeping political changes in Eastern Europe, the clock was set back to 11:50. This is encouraging: ten minutes is more than three. But there is an obverse side to this picture. In spite of the fact that even the most vociferous hawks in the U.S. admit that the "Soviet threat" has receded, no readiness is apparent on the American side to stop the qualitative arms race. For example, the Geneva Non-proliferation Treaty review conference ended in failure of agreement by the United States to effect a comprehensive test ban on nuclear weapons. In the U.S., the changes in the Soviet Union and in Eastern Europe tend to be hailed as a "victory for our side." But a victory is usually not regarded as an occasion for demanding change. A case in point is the recent statement by President Bush to the effect that now "more than ever" it is imperative to go ahead with the development of weapons in space.

What rationale can be offered in support of this astonishing position? Against what or whom are weapons in space supposed to "protect" the United States? Is everything that has happened in the Soviet Union and in the Warsaw Pact countries a vast charade to lull the U.S. into a false sense of security, while a Pearl Harbor-type attack is being stealthily prepared? Or is the development of a nuclear arsenal in a Third World country imminent, together with means of delivering nuclear warheads across an ocean?

If we insist on contemplating the "worst scenario," should we not rather consider the more likely possibility that a Third World country intent on destroying the United States would direct its efforts to developing a genocidal weapon other than a transcontinental missile, say a chemical or a biological weapon far cheaper to produce and deliver? The conclusion is inescapable that rationales offered for continuing to develop new weapons of the sort produced in the now obsolete Cold War cannot be taken at face value. They cannot be regarded as rational justifications of policy. Rather such rationales are manifestations of massive inertia in ways of thinking. Unfortunately, buzz words like "security," "defence," "deterrence," "balance of power," "vulnerability," "strategic advantage" are still legal currency in formulations of policy in spite of the fact that there is nothing to back them up in the way of references to reality. They have lost all meaning in the new situation.

The United States and the New Europe

The transfiguration of the political scene in Europe notwithstanding, plans for the "defence of Europe" are still on the drawing boards of the Pentagon. To be sure, they are being "revised," apparently to reflect awareness of the changes. Let us look at some of these "revisions."

From Paul Wolfowitz, an under-secretary of defence: "We are looking at revising a great many fundamental assumptions." Apparently, the reaction time of the U.S. war machine is being lengthened. The state of U.S. military preparedness against attack is now to be designed around a "14 day warning of Soviet preparedness to invade Europe. Glasnost and better intelligence suggest that it could be expanded to two or three months."[1]

Weapons development continues to be driven by institutional inertia. A new plan designated SIOP 7 has been in preparation since 1988. It amounts to a strategy for fighting a nuclear war with the Soviet Union by weapons designed to penetrate the deepest underground bunkers so as to "decapitate" the entire Soviet leadership. In a book published in 1990 we read:

The range of technologies currently under study is very wide and includes both directed and kinetic energy weapons. The first of these includes laser, neutral and charged particle beams and radio frequency beams. The kinetic energy weapons are the kind we are already used to, but they now come with precision guidance and will soon have the very high velocities provided by electromagnetic propulsion. All of these weapons will eventually have the option of space-basing to increase their versatility and hence they all promise, or threaten, new military options.[2]

One of the striking facts of the present is that the leadership of the Soviet Union has become keenly aware of the dangers that threaten everyone, not just the power of the Soviet state. Moreover, it has acted on this recognition by radically altering the political complexion of that country to clear the way for coping with the global threats. This change of policy has had dramatic repercussions that have completely altered the complexion of the erstwhile Soviet empire.

Apparently, however, no analogous conspicuous change has taken place in the perceptions or actions of U.S. leadership. The

U.S. has recently projected the testing of nuclear weapons to the middle of the next century. We believe that this ossification of thinking is a major obstacle in the way of coming to grips with the paramount issues. As long as Canada's foreign policy remains linked to that of the United States, this backward kind of thinking stands in the way of Canada's contribution to a concerted effort to solve global problems.

The Disease: Conceptual Inertia or Addiction?

Just because any conceivable realistic justification for war plans has disappeared does not mean that war preparations can stop of their own accord. Directed action must be taken to stop them. Such action may require considerably less effort, organization, and expertise than was required to develop war preparations. Nevertheless so long as sufficient political will to effect a radical change of policy is lacking, war preparations will continue.

Inertial thinking is often rooted in a so-called unfalsifiable assumption – something that is assumed to be true regardless of evidence against it. Such an assumption is illustrated by the story about a mental patient who was convinced that he was dead. A psychiatrist tried to reason with him. "Do you agree," he asked the patient, "that dead men don't bleed?" "Yes, I know that," said the patient. "Would you let me prick your finger to see if you bleed? If you are dead, you shouldn't bleed, should you?" The patient agreed. So his finger was pricked and, of course, a drop of blood came out. "What do you say to that?" asked the psychiatrist. The patient looked embarrassed. "I was wrong, doctor," he said, "dead men do bleed."

Mental inertia is due not only to difficulty of changing established mental habits. It can serve also to preserve institutions in which people have vested interests. Such are the institutions that have grown up in all countries on the foundation of "national defence."

The foundation consists not only of military establishments but also of their adjuncts – the war industries, the research institutes and think tanks, the stimuli to the economy in the form of contracts, jobs, etc. It has also a solid ideational base at the centre of which, analogous to a deity at the centre of a religion, is an image of the Enemy. The defence policies of most European states since the establishment of the present system of sovereign states (in the Treaty of Westphalia in 1648) were often based on a specific designated enemy. Denmark and Sweden were each other's designated enemies for centuries, as were Sweden and Russia, Russia and Turkey, England and Holland, Prussia and France. Because of shifting alliances and power relations, the general staffs of major military powers developed contingent plans for operations against any of several hypothetical enemies, usually bordering states. In this way, a constant state of war readiness was maintained. And this very war readiness, that is, awareness of it in others, provided its own justification.

After World War II, the Hobbesian-Clausewitzian system of continual potential war of every one against every one disintegrated in Europe. It became impossible to get the people of England to support a war against Holland or the people of Germany to support a war against France, the traditional enemy. Nevertheless, the war system comprising armies, war industries, espionage, etc. remained intact in Europe. It was maintained in the West by the spectre of a new formidable designated enemy, namely, the Soviet Union. All scenarios, many acted out in maneuvers, assumed the same alignment of forces: the "Communist empire" against the "Free World."

In the United States, the spectre was adorned by all possible combinations of hypothetical enemies. In the age of unlimited mobility, these were no longer confined to bordering states. The United States, with only two border states at its disposal, had to give rein to its military imagination. For example, the U.S. Institute of Land Combat was given the task of planning several hundred possible wars involving combinations of states, some hypothetical allies, others hypothetical enemies. Because all combinations were hypothetical, the number of possible alliances provided material for decades of "productive" work. A sampling submitted by the Institute of Land Combat gives an idea of the limits to which military imagination will go:

. . . U.S., Yugoslavia, and Italy vs. Soviet Union, Bulgaria, and Hungary; U.S. allied with Norway, West Germany, and Denmark vs. U.S.S.R., East Germany, Poland, and Finland; U.S., allied with Libya (sic!), Tunisia, Italy and West Germany vs. United Arab Republic, U.S.S.R., and Algeria.[3]

Although the various combinations are purely hypothetical, (one suspects that the main purpose of these exercises is to keep strategists busy), the underlying basis of all these imaginary wars is the confrontation of the superpowers. It now appears, however, that the Soviet Union is no longer willing to serve as the Designated Enemy. The war institution can be kept alive either by insisting that the Soviet Union can resume its prescribed role or by identifying new enemies, be they terrorists, insurgents, drug peddlers, or commercial rivals playing with the idea of becoming military powers.

There is a tradition in industrialized countries, nurtured by conceptual inertia, that "creating jobs" is a vital goal of a good economic policy. This idea is easy to accept since unemployment is a chronic disease of the "free enterprise" economies and is frequently a vital political issue. One of the characteristics of inertial thinking is that means are frequently transformed into ends. This is a natural consequence of the division of labour. In the performance of a complex task, each participant, preoccupied with doing his/her part, does not often see (or care to see) how this part is going to contribute to the achievement of the original goals of the task.

Creating jobs has become a goal, regarded desirable by all. What is lost sight of is the purpose of the economy itself for which jobs must be maintained or created. Of course, it will be readily agreed that the purpose of an economy is to provide goods and services that satisfy human needs. But this purpose does not figure in the goal of "creating jobs" as an end in itself. For example, war industries are said to be "good for the economy," because they provide jobs. When we stop to think what the war industries produce, we are forced to concede that the products serve their purpose if they are not used. In fact, if these products were ever used, we would be worse off than if they were not produced at all. Hence the war industries produce things that are at best useless.

Here the usual arguments are marshalled about the necessities of "deterrence" (if the products are not used) or of "defence" (if they are). These arguments, however, bristle with buzz words, which in the era of wars of total destruction have lost all meaning, as we have seen. If they are endowed with meaning, it is to serve a specific purpose – to rationalize the continued existence (and burgeoning growth) of the war system. The war system is defended because so many careers, livelihoods, ambitions, sources of power, sources of ego-gratifications, foundations of political viability, etc. depend on its continued existence.

The war system is like a parasitic organism that in the course of its evolution has adapted itself to its (also evolving) environment. The environment of a parasitic organism is its host. In this case, the environment is the society in which the war system is imbedded. The adaptation of a parasite to its habitat within the host is successful to the extent that the parasite mimics the host's tissues and so is tolerated by the host. This is especially true of malignant growths. The monstrously swollen military establishments of the nuclear age mimic the role of "protectors" of the societies in which they are imbedded, a role that their ancestors in bygone ages may have actually played.

Aside from the mimicry, there is another way in which parasites become adapted to their hosts. They can produce and nurture addiction. This can be seen especially vividly in the United States where the war system nurtures technolotry (worship of, or addiction to, technology). To see this, consider the transformation of the so-called martial virtues in the age of megatechnology. There was a time when these virtues consisted primarily of physical strength, bravery, and fierceness. Those times are gone. Strength, once needed to wield heavy weapons, is not needed to operate electronic equipment. Bravery, once needed to suppress the instinct of self-preservation on the battlefield, is not needed when the battlefield is no longer an arena where enemies meet face to face. Fierceness was needed to suppress the aversion against killing one's own kind. It is no longer needed when killing on the scale of millions is decomposed into hundreds of fractional jobs, none of which bears the slightest resemblance to killing.

If the traditional military virtues are gone, what are the presently appreciated military virtues? For such there must be if the war machine is to be kept going by human beings. However horrendous the results of what human beings serving the war machine do in the process of serving it, human beings must be motivated by feelings consistent with their self respect. It seems the strongest motivation in our age dominated by technology is the exercise of technical and organizational skills. And this is the way the war machine is run, especially in the United States. Already in World War II commanders of some air bases (those of the Air Transport Command) were air line executives rather than professional military officers. The Secretary of Defence in President Lyndon Johnson's administration had been president of Ford Motor Company. Witness the remarks made at a conference on national security. The excerpt is taken from a discussion of various criteria which, in the opinion of the authors, should be taken into account in the design of defence strategy. After criticizing some quantitative criteria as too crude, the authors propose a better criterion: the number and value of enemy targets that can be destroyed for a given budget.

This is a criterion that makes a little more sense. It takes into account not only the numbers of our offensive bombers and missiles but also their operational effectiveness . . . It still is, of course, an ambiguous criterion and requires more precise definition. For example, what target systems – population, industry, or military bases – should we use to keep score . . .?[4]

Substitute "sales volume increment per dollar spent" for "value of enemy targets" and the presentation becomes indistinguishable from that of a corporation officer discussing the pros and cons of mass advertising versus promotion campaigns in pushing a product. Note also the allusion to sport, another activity with a positive image: " . . . what target systems . . . should we use to keep score?" In adopting the practices and language of business (or sport), the institution of war adapts itself to a society which an American president characterized by a profound remark: "The business of America is business."

Obstacles to a Cure

We have depicted the war system as a parasitic organism causing a disease affecting all humanity. In searching for a cure, we might turn our attention to accumulated experience in dealing with diseases. This task has been traditionally performed by the medical profession. However, until the advent of scientific medicine, the contributions of the medical profession to the task of preventing, controlling, curing, or eradicating diseases were spotty. Setting broken bones, some primitive surgery, use of medicinal herbs marked the extent of effective traditional medical skills. Possibly among preliterate peoples, ritual and magic alleviated some mental and psychosomatic disorders by power of suggestion. When, however, we examine the medical practices in Europe from the Middle Ages until well into the nineteenth century, we could conjecture that during the whole period when medical "theory" was dominated by metaphysical speculations and outright superstition, physicians may have killed considerably more people than they cured.

With the advent of scientific research in areas relevant to medicine, the situation changed radically. Definitive cures were found for many diseases. Prevention of disease by hygienic measures became dramatically effective. Several diseases have been altogether eradicated. All these successes were based on discoveries of relationships between "causes" and "effects" – the sort of discoveries that characterize all substantive scientific research.

There is an important distinction between necessary and sufficient causes. An event A is called a sufficient cause of an event B, if B must occur whenever A occurs. An event A is called a necessary cause of an event B if event B cannot occur unless A occurs.

From the scientific point of view, both necessary and sufficient causes of disease are of interest, for the aim of any scientific research is (or ought to be) that of broadening our understanding of how and why things happen. From the practical point of view, however, that is, of someone who seeks in the first instance to find means of preventing, curing, or eradicating a disease, it suffices to know a necessary cause – a condition or event without which the disease could not occur. In the absence of *tubercle bacilli*, tuberculosis cannot occur. In the absence of vitamin C deficiency, scurvy cannot occur. Without certain specifiable genetic defects, certain handicaps cannot occur.

Applying the same reasoning to the problem of "curing the war disease," we see that even though from the scientific point of view both necessary and sufficient causes of wars are of interest, from the point of view of preventing wars or eradicating war altogether, only the necessary causes must be known — events, conditions, or processes, without which wars could not occur. It turns out that if we fix our attention on the sort of wars that presently threaten the very life of humanity, we see that a necessary cause of such a war is obvious, namely, the existence of weapons of total destruction. Arguments to the effect that, even if all weapons were eliminated, people would still fight with sticks and stones, because people are "by nature" aggressive, is not relevant in the present context. Fighting with sticks and stones does not endanger the survival of humanity. Nuclear, chemical, and biological weapons do.

There is a fundamental difference between the tasks of the medical researcher and those of the peace researcher. Necessary causes of various diseases are all different. In some cases it is a pathogenic organism; in others a dietary deficiency; in still others a genetic defect. Each disease presents a different problem. Once, however, a necessary cause of a disease is found, finding a specific cure is often only a step away. Most important, once an effective cure (or preventive measure) is found, the way to application is usually clear. Institutions exist willing, able, and empowered to implement the prescribed therapies or procedures, namely, the medical profession, boards of health, hospitals with their facilities and organization, and so on.

The peace researcher's position is quite different. In searching for necessary causes of wars, he/she is breaking through an open door. These are obvious, namely, weapons. The cure is, therefore, also obvious: the abolition of weapons or, more generally, the abolition of the war establishment, the institutions comprising the global war machine. The cause is known and the prescription follows. Thus, with respect to diagnosis, the peace researcher has an advantage over the medical researcher. It is with respect to implementation that the position of the peace researcher is incomparably more difficult than that of the medical researcher. There are no institutions that stand ready, willing, and empowered to implement the prescription. On the contrary, the institutions that mimic the protective function of the war machine stand ready, willing, and empowered to implement every new way of increasing the extent of destruction wreaked by weapons supposed to confer "security." The prospect of a cure by radical surgery is not bright. We must look to other kinds of therapy.

New Wine in Old Bottles

It is instructive to follow the fate of organisms and of parts of organisms in the course of evolution when there are changes in their environments. Three kinds of fate have been discerned.

(i)   *Extinction* — the organism, previously adapted to its environment, ceases to be adapted to a new environment. Example: the dinosaurs.

(ii)   *Prosperity* — the organism becomes especially well adapted to a new environment. Thereby it attains a reproductive advantage over its competitors and becomes dominant in some ecosystem. Example: the insects, now comprising more species than all other classes combined, illustrate especially successful adaptation.

(iii)   *Transformation of function* — this process is commonly observed in parts of organisms, for example their organs. The environment of an organ is the organism in which it is imbedded – its "host." The way of life of this host may be something to which the organ must become adapted. Thus, changes in the way of life of the organism can induce changes in the organ. Example: the bladder that many fishes used in propelling themselves up and down under water (by intake and expulsion of air) lost this function as fishes evolved into land-dwelling animals. But the "descendant" of the bladder survived by changing into a lung.

Analogous fates can be observed in institutions. An institution may become maladapted to a new social environment and disappear. It may become especially well adapted to a new social environment and prosper. Or it may survive in a new social environment by changing its function.

An example of extinction is provided by chattel slavery, which became maladapted in societies with advanced technologies.

An example of a successful adaptation is provided by institutionalized science, which has grown immensely in terms of personnel and resources. Unlike chattel slavery, science became especially well adapted to societies with rapidly developing advanced technologies.

An institution that was able to avoid extinction by changing its function was a charitable institution that provided assistance to settlers who struck out to the American West and failed to find homesteads, having met with misfortune (disease, attacks by natives, highwaymen, etc.). They returned to St. Louis, Missouri, the usual point of departure, broke. This pattern of settlement became extinct. The function, however, was able to survive. It now supports Travelers' Aid, performing a different but somewhat similar function by assisting travelers who get into difficulties and find themselves stranded in an airport, railway station or bus terminal in a strange city.

Transformation of function permits institutions to continue to exist when their existence can no longer be justified by their original function. This is important, because resistance against abolishing most established institutions is often formidable. For example, in spite of the fact that the Swiss army cannot possibly be expected to play a part in defending Switzerland against invasion (for lack of potential invaders or of any conceivable rationale for an invasion), the actual abolition of the army is not in prospect. It is still impossible to mobilize the political will of the nation to abolish this institution, as has been shown by a recent referendum on this issue. Nevertheless the fact that the issue has been brought up may be a harbinger of a changed environment. It is conceivable that abolition will be approved in a future referendum. It is also conceivable that the institution will survive by changing its function, for example, by expanding its present "side line" of providing a ceremonial guard for the Vatican.

Similarly, the abolition of the Canadian defence establishment is presently impossible, even though it can no longer discharge the traditional functions of an armed force. To be sure, the question, "Of what use are the Canadian forces?," can be answered by traditional assertions: "They are indispensable for the defence of the country; they serve to fulfill the obligations to our allies; they serve to preserve the values of the free world, etc." None of these phrases, however, can be referred to credible scenarios. The phrase "to defend our country" has no concrete meaning unless the question can be answered, "Against whom?" or, "Against what?." The phrase, "to help preserve the values of the free world," is meaningless unless the question can be answered, "What are those values and by whom or by what are they threatened and how can armed forces act so as to help preserve them?." To make meaningful the phrase ,"to fulfill the obligations to our allies," one must face and answer the question, "What are our allies up to?," or, "What are they likely to be up to that needs the participation of the Canadian forces?." Unless credible (not merely verbally coherent) scenarios can be offered to answer the above question, the conclusion is inescapable that the abolition of the Canadian armed forces is presently politically unthinkable only because it is impossible to mobilize the political will to do so regardless of whether they serve any rationally defensible function aside from maintaining themselves.

A way out of this impasse is suggested by the possibility of expanding the one function performed by the Canadian armed forces that can be discharged even if the global war machine is dismantled, namely, peace-keeping under sponsorship of a supranational body, such as the United Nations. In fact, this function is already becoming traditional in the Canadian armed forces. It contributes to the sort of leadership to which Canada should aspire in a world liberated from superpower confrontation. Such an adaptation would be another example of an institution surviving in a new environment by changing its function.

Indeed, transformation of function of present military establishments may be more desirable than their total extinction. The defence establishments have been repositories of skills and traditions which may be worth keeping alive. Among the skills are organizational competence required for any large-scale collective effort. Among the traditions are those embodied in certain "martial virtues" associated not so much with aggression and violence as with traits of character widely recognized as positive, for example, courage, self control, loyalty to a collective, etc.[5]

The difficulties of transforming the functions of present military establishments are of the same sort as those of abolishing them. Recommendations of this sort are based on a tacit assumption that a society is an autonomous decision maker and a free agent, able to structure itself in accordance with needs perceived in the light of insights induced by rational analysis. This assumption is questionable. Institutions imbedded in a society are systems often endowed with impressive viability potential, which enables them not only to withstand encroachments on their existence but also to resist attempts to change their character. Military establishments have acquired this immunity to a considerable degree. The threat of a cataclysmic end of civilization stems from this acquired autonomy and immunity.

III. THE THREAT OF AN END WITH A WHIMPER

The Population Explosion

Explicit warnings about inevitable depletion of resources were sounded two centuries ago when T. Malthus pointed out that a population increasing at a constant rate per capita must eventually outgrow the available food supply if arable land increases only by constant increments per unit time. Eventually, he held, if population growth were not stemmed "voluntarily," i.e., by abstention (the only method Malthus could think of), it would be stemmed by mass starvation.[6]

During the next century and a half massive increases in agricultural productivity seemed to refute Malthus' dire prediction. But it is now taken seriously. Mass starvation is already upon us. There is little doubt that the problem can be alleviated only if it is attacked from three sides – by further increasing agricultural efficiency, by population control, and by a more equitable utilization of available land.

In the industrialized countries, population is already voluntarily controlled. Two circumstances make this possible: first, almost universal availability of means of birth control and relatively easy spread of information about it; second, the motivation to limit family size. Both of these circumstances are directly related to the relative affluence of the industrialized world. Most people can afford to buy birth control devices. Moreover, the relative affluence nurtures consumer appetites and presents opportunities to both men and women for pursuing remunerative careers. Finally, old age no longer entails expectations of eventual dependence on children for support. Hence there is less motivation for raising large families. Therefore it seems that a reasonably sure way of stimulating voluntary family limitation is to raise the standard of living in impoverished countries. Only in this way can we be reasonably sure that: 1) information about effective means of birth control will be sufficiently widely disseminated; 2) birth control devices will be reasonably affordable; 3) motivation to raise large families will decrease (if other kinds of support for the aged are available); 4) motivation to limit family size will increase if career opportunities open up.

Despoliation and Degradation of the Planet

Aside from the old threat of population explosion, now revived, new threats are forcing themselves on human awareness. Unlike the population explosion, these are not "self-corrective" in the way the population explosion is (by mass starvation). That is to say, the threatened disasters may be irreversible. These are of two kinds, quantitative and qualitative. The former can be called despoliation threats, entailing simple exhaustion of: (a) food resources; (b) mineral resources; and (c) energy resources. The latter can be called degradation threats. These are degradation of: (a) the atmosphere; (b) the hydrosphere; (c) the geosphere; (d) the biosphere; (e) the noosphere. The atmosphere, the hydrosphere, and the geosphere refer respectively to the gaseous, liquid and solid jackets surrounding the core of our planet. The biosphere is the layer of living matter, now recognized as a vital component of the environment on which human life depends. The noosphere refers to a new concept – the total knowledge, true and false, beliefs, concepts, ideologies, accumulated through the ages of human experience.

Despoliation of Food Resources

Malthus' dire prediction seems about to be realized but not for the reason he stated. At this time, the world population has not outstripped available food supply. More food is now produced per capita than ever before in human history. Specifically, in 1985, 500 kilos of food was grown for every person then alive.

This does not mean, however, that this food is available to every person. In that year there were 730 million people without enough food to function normally.[7] Since 1985 the situation has deteriorated still further. The number of people on deficient diets in the Third World is now about 950 million. This constitutes a fifth of the world population.[8]

We have starvation in the midst of plenty. The reasons for this are many. In some regions too little food is grown. In some enough is grown, but many families do not have enough money to buy enough food. Even over-production of food has contributed to starvation by impoverishing the soil. The cities of the Third World are teaming with unemployed, particularly those who have migrated from rural to urban areas. In Manila, for example, low birth weight was found to be five times more frequent in the slums than in the planned residential areas. The question arises, "Why do these poor people migrate to the metropolises?." They leave the countryside because the food situation there is even worse. It is especially bad for people without enough land to grow food on. In Bangladesh, for example, the caloric intake of landless or near-landless households was found to be 1925 calories per person per day. In households owning more than seven hectares, the intake was 2375 calories. This latter figure is about the United Nations estimated minimal caloric intake for healthy humans.[9]

We discuss these trends under despoliation of food resources rather than under depletion, because the increase in starvation is not simply a manifestation of the Malthusian effect. As we have seen, in the past twenty years, the volume of food production has actually exceeded the demand. The breakdown of food consumption among the rich and the poor has revealed that the per capita food consumption of the poor has declined and therefore the per capita consumption of the rich has increased. As we shall see below, this is a direct effect of greed: arable land that could feed people who live on it is converted to yield crops (coffee, cotton, bananas) for export. In whatever way cash for export crops is distributed (and it is reasonable to suppose that the rich get the bigger cut), the bottom line is more starvation. This is what we mean by inequitable utilization of available land.

Despoliation of Energy Resources

Petroleum is a typical non-renewable resource. While the total amount of petroleum on the planet is not known, future availability can be estimated on the basis of presently known resources. At the present rate of consumption, the proven world oil reserves are sufficient for about thirty years. As in the case of food resources, this prospect can be attributed to despoliation. There is a crass disproportion in the consumption level of energy resources between the rich and the poor. The United States continues to lead the world in the consumption of oil followed by the U.S.S.R. and Japan. To be sure, these rates are related to the large populations of those countries. A more relative measure of consumption is the intensity of consumption – how much energy it takes to produce a unit of, say, the gross national product. By these standards, Canada leads the world, followed by the United States.[10] Consumption is considerably lower in the Third World, for example, in West Africa, by a factor of three or four.

The threatened exhaustion of energy resources can also be attributed to despoliation through inefficient use. The personal automobile, practically universal in the affluent world, is a conspicuous culprit. In this respect, the waste is more conspicuous in the United States and Canada. The large distances between populated centres in North America in comparison with Europe and Japan is partly but not entirely the cause of the promiscuous use of the private automobile. Another factor is the dominance of individualism in American life, in this case addiction to private comforts and the attendant neglect of public welfare. The automobile has been the primary factor in the deterioration of public transport in Canada and in the U.S., while such transport still functions well in Europe and Japan.

Some progress has been made here and there in the industrialized countries in changing attitudes toward promiscuous energy consumption. The changes can be attributed primarily to the sudden price increase of oil in the early 1970s. Between 1975 and 1985 conservation measures in the OECD countries reduced per capita energy use by 5%, while the per capita GDP grew 32%. More significantly, the trend shattered the widely held belief that economic growth necessitates increased energy use. Once the idea "takes," energy conservation is something everyone can participate in.

Whether the idea "takes" or not depends in large measure on policy. It is instructive to compare patterns of energy use in Texas and in California from 1977 to 1984. In Texas, where no incentives were introduced by the government to conserve energy, per capita energy use increased during those years at an average rate of 1.7% per year. In California, where strict energy conservation standards were adopted, energy consumption decreased in the same period at an average rate of 0.5% per year. Because energy conservation can be realized by appropriate policies, we can speak of despoliation of energy resources if such policies are not adopted.[11]

Dependence on non-renewable energy resources, as well as a failure to adopt and implement conservation policies, can be traced to preoccupation with profit rather than with human welfare. Renewable or virtually inexhaustible sources of energy – solar, geothermal, etc. – are available. What is required to be able to utilize them is direction of resources to appropriate scientific research, conversion of energy producing and energy consuming industries, and dissemination of information. For example, solar energy generated by photovoltaic cells presently costs about five dollars per "peak-watt" compared with between one and two dollars, the cost of conventional electricity. This comparison makes it appear as if the cost of solar energy is still prohibitive. However about ten years ago, solar energy cost about 600 dollars per "peak watt."[12]

Thermal current generators convert solar energy even more efficiently. Installations collecting solar energy near Los Angeles produce electricity at 9.3 cents per kilowatt-hour (in 30 MW reactors) and at 8 cents per kilowatt-hour (in 80 MW reactors). At this cost they are already attractive alternatives to installations using fossil fuels.

In view of these developments, could we not expect that solar energy at a competitive price may become available in a few years, at any rate before the known oil reserves are exhausted? If so, does it not seem worthwhile to launch energetic research efforts aimed at developing solar energy technology? Failure to undertake and implement these measures reflects lack of incentives in institutions able to do so.

An obstacle to significant progress in developing renewable or inexhaustible and environmentally safe sources of energy is preoccupation with the development of nuclear energy. The safety of nuclear reactors is a subject of controversy. Indisputable are the hazards to the environment generated by nuclear mining and waste products. At present, production of nuclear energy is by no means economically efficient. The emphasis on this alternative to fossil fuels can be attributed to the opportunity it provides for retaining centralized control of energy sources and, significantly, to the linkage between civilian and military uses of nuclear energy.

Degradation of the Atmosphere

The greatly increased concentration of carbon dioxide in the atmosphere (released through burning fossil fuels) is presently assumed to generate the so-called "greenhouse effect," a projected rise in the average temperature of the planet by some degrees. The magnitude of the effect, indeed its existence, is still a subject of controversy among scientists. However, the possibility of the projected effect is disputed by no one, and the possibility already constitutes a threat.

A rise of only a few degrees can have disastrous consequences for hundreds of millions of people, most of them already living in abject poverty. According to forecasts based on evidence currently available the temperature of the planet may rise by 2 °C in the course of the next 50 years and may continue to rise as the 21st century progresses if the present situation persists. To get an idea of the significance of this process, consider that since the end of the last glacial period, some 18,000 years ago, the average temperature of the planet rose only about 5 °C. To get an idea of the possible consequences of warming, consider that a rise of sea level of one or two metres (which is forecast) would inundate huge areas. Maumoon Abdul Gayoom, the president of the Republic of Maldives in the Indian Ocean, has declared the republic to be an "endangered nation."[13] Low-lying Pacific islands would simply disappear; large areas of Egypt and Bangladesh would be flooded, forcing up to 30 million people to become refugees. Many major ports would be inundated.

Besides unprecedented floods, drastic climatic changes are expected as consequences of the greenhouse effect. Unlike the floods, however, these effects cannot be predicted with comparable confidence. Some countries, for example, Canada and the Soviet Union, whose territories are in the high latitudes, may even gain as a result of warming, permitting agriculture where none was feasible before (assuming that those regions do not become drier). But other large agricultural areas may be destroyed. At any rate, rapid climatic change will probably result in disruptions in food supply with unforeseen social consequences.[14]

The depletion of the ozone layer has been as widely publicised as the warming effect. It is the layer in the atmosphere that protects the planet from the destructive effects of ultraviolet radiation from the sun. The danger became apparent when a "hole" was discovered in the ozone layer over Antarctica. The "hole" has appeared every spring since 1979. The ozone-poor air spread from the Antarctica over southern Australia and New Zealand. Around the world, the average reduction of ozone in the atmosphere has amounted to about 2% in the past twenty years, faster than had been predicted.

It seems the principal cause of ozone depletion is the emission of chloro-fluoro-hydrocarbons (CFC's) into the atmosphere. Some measures have been taken to forestall the danger generated by promiscuous use of CFC's. In 1987, 24 countries (mostly industrialized) signed a protocol in Montreal committing themselves to reducing the production of CFC's by half.

The severe problem associated with voluntary measures of this sort is illustrated by the refusal of China and India to sign the protocol. The argument supporting the refusal was that the countries of the Third World should not be penalized for the depletion of the ozone layer for which the industrialised countries are responsible. Here we see the tragic impasse resulting from a clash between conceptions of "justice" and a pragmatic approach to global problems. The argument that the rich countries are responsible for the aggravated danger and therefore should be "made to pay" carries some force. But the "justice" of the argument does not solve the problem. Even if the contribution of the Third World countries to the pollution of the atmosphere by CFC's is negligible, their refusal to participate in a common effort to cope with the danger undermines the spirit of cooperation, which alone offers some hope of saving the planet for posterity. The inescapable conclusion is that problems of environmental protection cannot be separated from problems of development arising in the Third World.

One way of countering the impasse is to make the technology of producing CFC substitutes, now being developed in industrialised countries, available at little or no cost to the developing countries. Presently it is China that can most undermine the international control effort. It has now embarked on a development programme that is quite modest by any standard of the affluent world but presents a serious danger to the environment. The plan is to put a refrigerator in every Chinese home by the year 2000. This would put China in the big league of

CFC producers with an output greater than that of the United States today. Should the Chinese forego the "luxury" of refrigerated food? If they will not, the responsibility for further degradation of the ozone layer will not be theirs alone. Western and Japanese companies are now supplying China with obsolete equipment with which to make refrigerators. This means profits. Supplying the Chinese with new technology for making CFC substitutes at prices they can afford does not.

The problem illustrates the linkage between environmental and social justice issues. Few would begrudge the Chinese their striving to bring their standard of living up to a level now technically available. But it appears that such a programme entails a danger of an environmental catastrophe. Are the Chinese to be induced to forego even a modest improvement in their lives because of the danger such an improvement poses, even though the problem arose because the affluent world had recklessly contributed to the degradation of the atmosphere? Responsibility to a global community can be expected to be felt only in consequence of integration into the world community, and this can be done only if the living standards of the impoverished become comparable to those of the affluent. How can this vicious cycle be broken?

Degradation of the Hydrosphere and the Geosphere

Degradation of water resources has attracted more attention than any other form of pollution. There is something especially frightening about poisons in water. In the Middle Ages scapegoats (e.g. Jews, Gypsies) were routinely accused of poisoning wells. In our time pollutants in water are increasingly widespread, identifiable, and traceable to human activity.

In the industrialised world "point source" pollution is traceable to a particular source, say an industrial plant; "non-point source" pollution means pollution that enters waters from sources other than municipal sewage treatment plants and industrial waste. In developing countries the distinction between point and non-point pollution is blurred, because most sewage and industrial waste there remains untreated.

In North America by far the most important source of fresh water pollution is agriculture. In the United States farm runoff accounts for 64% of pollution in rivers and 58% in lakes. Pesticides are now a contamination factor in the ground waters of 40 to 50 states. The world pesticide market reached an estimated $18 billion in 1987. Pesticide data for Europe and North America compiled by OECD in 1987 indicated a general increase over the past decade from 1% in Sweden (1976-84) to 127% in France (1975-82). Comparable increases occurred in the use of fertilizer, another important source of water pollution.[15]

The health hazards of contaminated water are serious. Excessive nitrates may cause blood poisoning in infants, tension in children, gastric cancers in adults and fetal malformations.

Urban non-point pollutants are contributed by storm runoff. This waste has been shown to be worse than treated sewage. Traffic emissions, construction, road de-icing, organic residues from vegetation and animals and atmospheric depositions produce growing amounts of sulphuric and nitric acid, copper, zinc, asbestos, etc.

Degradation of water has probably stimulated more energetic counter-measures than any other form of environmental degradation. Point source (industrial plants, etc.) are comparatively easier to deal with because responsibility for pollution can be pinpointed. Control of non-point pollution entails affecting agricultural policies and many other activities. Accordingly these controls present political difficulties. Ideally a country would establish a national policy or programme to assure comprehensive planning and institutional coordination. Few countries have done this.

The problem of controlling pollution becomes even more difficult when cooperation among countries is called for. A case in point is the acid rain problem, which involves both Canada and the United States, both as contributors and victims. Obviously unlimited national sovereignty is a major obstacle to solving problems of this sort.

Degradation of the hydrosphere is not confined to pollution. Addiction to megatechnology afflicted the Soviet Union throughout the seven decades of command economy. Aspiration to complete power over nature was a tenet of Soviet ideology ever since Lenin proclaimed that socialism meant Soviet power plus electrification. Since the Soviet Union is very rich in water, vast water management projects were planned to divert large volumes of water by changing the course of rivers. The rivers could supply the water needs of the nation fifteen times over. The trouble was that the rivers don't flow where the people are. The mighty rivers of Siberia flow north into the Arctic Ocean or east into the Pacific, while most of the people live in southern European Russia and in Central Asia. The scheme was to reverse the rivers to make them flow south. The plan was 15 years in the making and would shift 120 cubic kilometers of water per year to where it was needed.

Construction was already underway when in August 1988 the Central Committee of the Communist Party and the Council of Ministers of the Soviet Union stopped work pending "further study." The decision was a consequence of broad criticism of the plan. Opposition had surfaced already in 1983 when the Soviet Academy of Sciences Council for optimum planning and management met with the project's chief engineers and criticized the project on the basis of anticipated drastic environmental consequences. But that was before glasnost. In 1985, when the barriers to free speech and free press started to come down, the newspaper *Sovietskaya Rossiya* published pro and con stories on the project, as did the ecological journal *Priroda i Chelovek* (Nature and Man). Readers began writing in, most supporting the critics. (The Presidium of the Supreme Soviet receives more than 90,000 letters per year on environmental issues). In particular, voices were raised that the money could be better spent in cleaning up the heavily polluted rivers in southern Ukraine. A combination of expert advice and aroused public opinion succeeded in reversing a policy inspired by an arrogant attitude toward nature, which might have had disastrous consequences.

Degradation of the geosphere is a result of centuries of misuse of soils. Land degradation is as old as agriculture. Already in ancient Mesopotamia poor irrigation salinated vast areas. Until recently little thought was given to repairing damaged land. It has now become important to give some thought to this matter. It is practically certain that for some time at least the world population will continue to grow. People must be fed. It is soil that produces most nutrients. When population density was low, people, having exhausted the soil where they had settled, simply moved on. Even if they wanted to repair the damage, they could not, since they did not have the requisite technology. The situation has changed. Present day densities do not permit people to simply move on.

Fortunately some knowledge and some technology is available to repair damaged lands. This can be done in several ways. Traditionally lands were allowed to lie fallow to regenerate naturally. However, these practices required plentiful land. As land became scarce, fallow periods became shorter until they disappeared altogether. Repair can take two forms: restoration and rehabilitation. The former entails return of the soil to its natural state. The goal of rehabilitation is to make the soil productive again. Clearly where land is scarce, only rehabilitation is presently practicable.

Mountainous regions have particular problems. Dwellers in these regions fight gravity, since soil tends to slide downhill leaving bare rock. When vegetation and soil are depleted, agricultural production can decline rapidly and the threat of flooding in nearby lowlands increases. Engineering solutions such as check dams and terraces are sometimes effective but require maintenance.

A major form of land degradation is desertification, a process very difficult to combat. Drylands comprise presently 18% of the land area of developing countries. About 300 million people live on them. In many regions soil is eroding far faster than its normal rate. Poor farm management, overgrazing or overcultivation of land unsuitable for agriculture are among the major causes. A dramatic erosion catastrophe occurred in the United States in the 1930s, a consequence of despoliation of the forests, which exposed the land to seeping winds that simply carried the soil away. John Steinbeck's novel The *Grapes of Wrath* is about refugees from the "dust bowl" who were dispossessed by this degradation.

Degradation of soil has spiked the hopes raised in mid-century by the prospect of a "green revolution," based on the development of new strains of grains promising fabulous yields. The loss of arable land outstripped the gains in yield. The decline of per capita grainland since 1950 tells the story. From 1950 to 1960 the overall decline was 8%; in the next decade 11%, in the next 16%. A further decline of 15% is projected to the year 2000. A total of 50% loss of arable land coupled with a 100% increase of population in the last half of the present century may well wipe out any gains made by the "green revolution."

Degradation of the Biosphere

Unlike the dangers associated with the greenhouse effect, the depletion of the ozone layer, and pollution, there are others, generated by another kind of environmental degradation, not ordinarily appreciated by most people, since a deeper knowledge of biology is required to understand its nature.

Every kind of plant or animal alive today owes its existence to being adapted to the environment in which the species lives. The temperatures of its habitat varies within limits tolerated by it. The land, air, or water around it provide its food – the source of energy it uses to stay alive. If other organisms prey on it, it has ways of protecting itself. Although an individual of its kind can fall victim to a predator, there are enough surviving to produce successive generations.

These adaptations used to be thought of as deliberate arrangements made by Providence or some similar creative principle in order to enable creatures to continue to exist (collectively, if not individually). In the light of modern biology, we understand these adaptations differently. They now appear to be results of natural selection. The living things that we see around us are those that happened to become adapted to their environments. Those that did not adapt are not around.

Two principles govern the evolution of life forms. One is random variation; the other natural selection. Random variations are produced by minute changes in the hereditary substance of living organisms or by random combinations of hereditary units (genes) in the union of male and female gametes, which initiates reproduction. This provides the variety from which the most viable individuals are selected for further reproduction. It follows that genetic variety is indispensable for survival of living things. This is so because the environment does not stay put. It keeps changing. Organisms that were adapted to a given environment may no longer be adapted to a new environment. It is the variability of their genetic make-up that saves them from extinction.

The principle is well known to animal breeders. Long before the mechanisms of heredity were discovered, people bred dogs, horses and cattle to suit their purposes by controlling procreation. They thereby modified the anatomical, physiological, and even psychological features (the latter in dogs, for example) of these animals toward desirable types. Here the selection agency was human beings / homo sapiens. But the principle of environmental adaptation applies here as well, if we regard human beings / homo sapiens as part of the environment of the domesticated animal.

As the science of genetics developed, the same principle was applied to breeding plants. Disease resistant grains or pleasing varieties of flowers were developed. This shaping of plants and animals depended on the existence of "gene pools" in which a large variety of genetic material is stored.

Depletion of the gene pool is still another form of environmental degradation. A rain forest, for example, is an immensely rich gene pool, containing countless numbers of plant and animal species. A desert, in contrast, is an impoverished gene pool. It contains much more uniformity than diversity. Destruction of rain forests impoverishes the planet genetically. At present the Third World is the source of over one half of the genes of plants used in the developed world to improve agricultural species and (what is especially important) to develop medicines.[16]

Depletion of the world gene pool has been to a certain extent forestalled by the establishment of gene banks – refrigerated stores of genetic substances from which new crops and new medicines can be developed. In the last fifteen years, some forty such banks have been established, storing a great number of germplasm collections world wide. The establishment of these gene banks reflects a realization of the necessity to preserve the rich variety of the biosphere. The biosphere is a vast reservoir of supreme importance to human life. We have studied in a serious way only about one percent of the world's plants, even fewer of the world's animal species. It is hard to imagine what medical, industrial, and agricultural riches are being denied us by our ignorance. We do know that a single insect or plant may sometimes be the key to a whole ecological structure.

The thoughtless destruction of the Amazon rain forest has been recently publicised. That the attack on the rain forest is an attack on the entire biosphere (and therefore on humanity) is obvious. Forests (of which the rain forest is the richest sector) are the "lungs" of the planet. Only plants can convert the carbon dioxide exuded by animals back into oxygen that animals inhale. There is thus a vital symbiotic relationship between animals and plants. To destroy forests for short term benefit is as senseless as to burn a house down for a barbecue.

There is still another way to see the more subtle damage done by ruthlessly destroying the variability of the biosphere. It is generally realized that our behaviour is shaped by our attitudes. It is not so commonly realized that our attitudes are also shaped by our behaviour. A callous person thoughtlessly hurts others. But by repeatedly hurting others, perhaps at first unwillingly, a sensitive person may well become callous.

When we exploit the biosphere for short term gain, we not only jeopardize possible future benefits from a rich biosphere. We also become insensitive to the biosphere as an integral part of our collective life. The environmentalists and animal rights activists who make much of protecting commercially unimportant species (e.g. whooping cranes, rare snakes, etc.) are accused of "sentimentalism." Aside from the question of why "sentimentalism" should be disparaged, one can point out that these "sentimentalists" act as guardians of a certain *attitude* toward nature which in our present situation has genuine survival value. Just as respect for human life has survival value for the human race regardless of whatever utilitarian value may be attached to a particular life, so a feeling of respect, even reverence for nature, has survival value because it creates a certain climate that contributes to shaping collective behaviour. Respect for nature is induced by an esthetic appreciation of its richness and variability.

Degradation of Human Resources

The viability of the human race depends not only on available food, mineral, and energy resources but also upon human resources, in particular on the ability of people to participate in collective problem solving. This ability is impaired if the material welfare of people declines or is threatened. The degradation of our environment and of ourselves reinforce each other, accelerating our demise.

In what follows, we will mean by "wage earners" the large majority of people in the industrialized world who work for a living.

A relatively small proportion of these, professional and middle management personnel, have been able to maintain their economic position in Canada, but a large majority have not. Up until the 1970s the economic situation of the wage earners was improving, mainly because of an expanding economy and unionization. This gave workers bargaining power. Since then, however, their situation has been declining in consequence of growing unemployment and underemployment and a drop in real wages. Fundamental changes in the mode of production has led to a decline in unionized jobs on the labour market. The trend has not been simply a consequence of the recession in the 1970s. Even after the recession ended, the position of wage earners was not restored.

The disparity between the well-off and the poor generates a conflict of interests in an increasingly polarized population. While the "middle class" workers are able to maintain their economic status, which is the basis of social stability, the disadvantaged are not. The polarization is a major obstacle to collective effort in seeking and implementing solutions to major global problems, such as environmental protection, establishment of a lasting peace, and improving global social justice.

On the global scale, the polarization is conspicuous and severe. It can be regarded as a degradation of human resources. Besides undermining the motivation to do constructive work that contributes to the welfare of all, the degradation of human resources diverts human talent and efforts into destructive or parasitic activities (crime, serving the global war machine, etc.). A conspicuous example of such degradation is the global drug racket. Two circumstances provide conditions favourable to the rapid growth of this form of parasitism: the spread of addiction in the affluent world and concomitantly of drug traffic. The differential between the low cost of growing the plants and the huge returns goes to the criminal entrepreneurs. Because of the degree of organization required and of the dangers involved in intense competition in a lawless world, the most ruthless, reckless, and aggressive are recruited into this activity. Drug trafficking has now become an important component of global terrorism. In Columbia, the drug lords commanding private armies have challenged the state itself. The large profits enable them to equip their armies with modern sophisticated weapons. In the United States armed gangs patrol neighbourhoods to protect monopolies for their bosses. Governments have been corrupted by the lucrative profits.

The increase of this form of parasitism has been most dramatic during the last twenty years. In Peru and Bolivia, coca leaf production has increased seven fold in that time. The harm done is not confined to addicts. In Guatemala, poppy production, previously rare, has displaced food production in thousands of hectares of land, converting diversified agriculture to single cash crop agriculture with the well know deleterious effects.

Much is made of this blight in the media and by governments, particularly in the U.S., which has even planned military operations against drug cartels. However, the conspicuousness of this form of parasitism should not blind us to other forms that are "legal" but no less destructive.

Any exploitation of human resources, either in the classical sense of exploiting human labour for the enrichment of a privileged group or, as is becoming more widespread, in the form of channeling human effort and ingenuity into essentially destructive activities, amounts to degradation of human resources. Consider the harm done by the tobacco industry, the waste of human resources by the war industries, the contribution to killings of human beings by the global arms trade. The struggle against the degradation of human resources must be conducted on the broadest front since this form of degradation is a component of all others.

Degradation of the Noosphere

In addition to the material layers surrounding our planet, we can discern an "immaterial" one – the noosphere, the collective mind of humanity. No mystical significance needs to be attached to this concept. By the "collective mind" we mean simply the sum total of knowledge (true and false), ideas, beliefs, attitudes, etc., components of global culture, which, although they are "emanations" from the human component of the biosphere, constitute a system in their own right. For instance, languages clearly belong to this sphere, and they exhibit characteristics of evolution strikingly similar to biological evolution – differentiation of dialects, languages, families of languages, etc., analogous to the differentiation of species, genera, classes, and phyla in the biosphere. Similarly, systems of philosophy, ideologies, scientific disciplines, art forms, and religions all undergo evolution and so induce changes in the noosphere.

From a given ideological standpoint some of these changes are regarded as progressive, others as regressive. In the light of the global problems singled out here, it is clear that some prominent changes in the noosphere should be regarded as regressive. The most conspicuous of these is the hypertrophy of ideational systems totally devoted to the struggle for power, whether in the context of business competition or of rapacious exploitation of resources without regard for the long-term consequences, or, most clearly, in the military sphere. We are reminded of Arnold Toynbee's insight into the nature of a response produced by a culture to a challenge. If the challenge is weak, for example, in an environment that provides an easy livelihood, so is the response. As a result, the culture lacks vitality or dynamism. If, on the contrary, the challenge is extremely severe, the culture survives by a tour-de-force, channeling all of its energies into meeting the challenge and becoming impoverished in the process. Toynbee cites Sparta as an example of a culture that succumbed to its own tour-de-force, the achievement of superior military organization by means of which the Spartans kept the Helots (a conquered people) in submission. Sparta has produced nothing else in the way of cultural heritage, while the culture of Athens still lives in the soul of western civilization.

Pursuit of even more power against either real or imagined enemies or against the challenge of nature may be a tour-de-force which is degrading the noosphere, the unique survival mechanism of the human race.

IV. THE THREAT OF PERPETUAL VIOLENCE

Since the end of World War II there have been no major wars among the nations of the affluent world. Mass killing, however, has continued in the Third World. Estimated war-related deaths from 1945 to 1989 number almost 30 million. A large majority of these deaths were of civilians. The following figures for 1989 compiled by R.L. Sivard[17] on the "twelve most unfortunate countries" tell the story.

Table 1

Military and civilian deaths in twelve selected countries in 1989
(after Sivard, 1989)

Country	Military deaths	Civilian deaths
Afghanistan	55,000	670,000
Sudan	6,000	500,000
Mozambique	50,000	365,000
Uganda	8,000	300,000
Guatemala	38,000	100,000
Ethiopia	39,000	500,000
El Salvador	18,000	47,000
Lebanon	22,000	40,000
Angola	25,000	30,000
Peru	5,000	10,000
Sri Lanka	5,000	4,000
Iraq	1,000	9,000
Total	272,000	2,575,000

Civilian deaths outnumber military by more than 9 to 1. Routine slaughter of civilians in modern warfare had already started before World War II, namely, in China (by the Japanese) and in the Spanish civil war (by Germans and Italians). Guernica, etched in human memory by Picasso, became the symbol of those massacres. During World War II enemy industry became a "legitimate target" providing an excuse for bombing of cities and the indiscriminate killing of civilians. But already in 1940 this excuse was dropped. Enemy "morale" became the target in the terror bombings of Coventry, Rotterdam, Hamburg, Dresden, Hiroshima, and Nagasaki.

Interventions

The killing of civilians can be partly attributed to the nature of modern weapons, particularly the bomber plane. Since 1945, however, another factor, the intervention of industrialized states in the wars of the Third World has become important. The developed nations intervened by sending troops and by supplying the warring factions with weapons.

The use of troops has had two goals. One was to preserve the dominance of industrialized countries over the developing countries. For instance, the thirty year war of the twentieth century (the war in Southeast Asia) amounted to a war waged first by France, then by the United States against countries struggling to emerge from colonial status: Vietnam, Cambodia, and Laos. The proxy war waged by the United States against Nicaragua was also primarily a neo-colonial war. The Soviet intervention in Afghanistan was an attempt to establish political hegemony on the fringes of the Soviet empire.

The second goal of intervention was to rehearse for World War III without risking total war and destruction of the home lands, much as Nazi Germany and Fascist Italy used Spain as a rehearsal area. The Third World paid most of the blood price in those wars.

The supply of war technology (responsible for the magnitude of the slaughter) has been motivated by the appetite for profit but in many instances was also related to the Cold War. Supplying a developing country with war material is an effective way of keeping it within one's own sphere of influence as a client state. Arms exports dictated by such strategic considerations have been characterized primarily by one-sidedness. Only the country or faction on the "right side" of the Cold War was supplied, e.g., Pakistan and not India by the U.S., the central Ethiopian government and not the insurgents by the Soviet Union, the insurgents and not the central government in Angola by the U.S. Export of arms motivated purely by profit has been impartial, as in the case of France supplying both sides of the Iran-Iraq war. In both "ideological" and "non-ideological" military aid, the bottom line has always been slaughter, including, in large measure, slaughter of civilians.

With the drying up of the Cold War, the case for intervention based on geopolitical considerations has collapsed. Since the withdrawal from Afghanistan, the Soviet Union has lost whatever interest it might have had in imperial expansion and could not pursue it successfully, even if it wanted to; communist ideology and economics have lost their appeal even in the Soviet Union. The Soviets have abandoned control of their former satellites and they have instituted domestic reforms within their own country. No longer strategic assets in the global geopolitical struggle, sources of vital materials and land for military bases, Third World countries have become irrelevant or marginal assets.

If the momentum of the disintegration of the Cold War continues, interventions that have characterized U.S. behaviour in the Third World also seem likely to wither under the heat of public and Congressional scrutiny.

However, new militant regimes bent on conquest and apparently commanding fervent support by their populations at least initially present a new source of acute danger. The attack of Iraq on Kuwait has infused morbid hopes in U.S. intervention enthusiasts. Caspar Weinberger, former U.S. Secretary of

Defence, wrote as follows during the rapidly developing crisis in the Middle East:

In 1984 while I was Secretary of Defense, I proposed several "tests" governing a situation in which United States should – and could effectively– commit armed forces to combat. By these criteria Iraq's invasion of Kuwait qualifies as a clear-cut case calling for U.S. military intervention. And perhaps for the first time since before the Vietnam War, optimum political conditions also exist for effective action.[18]

Weinberger then proceeds to list these "optimum" conditions: (1) U.S. vital interests must be at stake; (2) there must be reasonable assurance of public support; (3) there must be clearly defined military objectives that can be secured; (4) U.S. must have the capability to achieve success; (5) U.S. forces must be committed only as a last resort. He goes on to point out with satisfaction that all these conditions are now at hand. Noting with approval the multilateral economic sanctions, the nearly unanimous U.N. vote supporting a world-wide boycott, etc., he notes, nevertheless that

. . . behind all the multilateral actions, boycotts and diplomatic maneuverings, the crucial factor is that the U.S. stands ready to take unilateral military action. As he darkly ponders his next move, Saddam should not doubt that he is facing an America ready, willing and capable of committing our forces to combat and winning.[19]

Assuming that the United States could destroy Saddam Hussein (which might involve the destruction of millions of civilians), the global political costs of such an intervention would be horrendous. The U.S., as an embodiment of the Rambo image, would be confirmed in the role of an international outlaw no less than Iraq. The momentum toward disarmament would be lost. The Pentagon would regain its position as the fountainhead of American foreign policy. Worst of all, the unprecedented opportunity would be missed together in serving a common cause. Of course, it would take longer for a worldwide boycott to spike the ambitions of the new bully than an outright war, but the rewards of collective non-violent coercion would be immense. These rewards would be embodied not only in the growing prestige of the United Nations as a peace keeping force but also in the experience of organizing, implementing, and monitoring the boycott as an effective non-violent weapon against aggression. It may be sad to admit that the basis of cooperation is all too frequently the perception of a common enemy, but there is no reason why the present opportunity should not be utilized to teach nations to cooperate without paying the exorbitant price of war. The sort of world that emerged from the "victory" over the Axis should serve as a warning to the enthusiasts of military intervention (especially unilateral) no matter how it may seen justified in the short run.

Violence Instigated by Environmental Issues

The potential of massive violence in the Third World will by no means be dissipated by the establishment of peace in the affluent world alone. Awareness of environmental dangers, coupled with an awareness of the affluence enjoyed by the First World can aggravate the conflicts on the fringes of the latter. We will illustrate the nature of these dangers by two examples.

On January 13, 1990, Turkey began filling the giant reservoir behind the new Attaturk dam in south-eastern Anatolia. Turkey announced that for one month it would hold back the main flow of the Euphrates River on the dam, and thus effectively cut the downstream flow within Syria to about a quarter of its normal rate.[20] By early in the next century, Turkey plans to build a huge complex of over twenty dams and irrigation systems along the upper reaches of the Euphrates. This $21 billion Great Anatolia project, if fully funded and built, will reduce the annual average flow of the Euphrates within Syria from 32 billion cubic metres to 20 billion. Moreover, the water that passes through Turkey's irrigation systems and on to Syria will be laden with fertilizers, pesticides, and salts.

Syria is already desperately short of water, with an annual water availability of only about 600 cubic metres per capita.[21] Almost all of the water for its towns, industries, and farms comes from the Euphrates. Furthermore, Syria's population growth rate – at 3.7% per year – is one of the highest in the world, and this will add further impetus to the country's demand for water.

Turkey and Syria have exchanged angry threats over this situation. Syria gives sanctuary to guerillas of the Kurdish Workers Party (the PKK), which has long been waging an insurgency against the Turkish government in eastern Anatolia. Turkey suspects that Syria might use these separatists to gain leverage in bargaining over Euphrates water. Thus, in October, 1989, Prime Minister Ozal suggested that Turkey might impound the river's water if Syria did not restrain the PKK. Although he later retracted this threat, the tensions have not been resolved, and there are currently no high-level talks on water sharing. There is, therefore, a real possibility of a violent confrontation over Euphrates water sometime in the near future.

Our next example concerns festering insurgent movements chronic throughout the Third World.

As recently as World War II, about half the area of the Philippines was forested. Since then, logging and the encroachment of farms has reduced this expanse of virgin and second-growth forest from about 16 million hectares to between 6.8 and 7.6 million.[22] Whereas at the turn of the century, the Philippines had about 10 million hectares of virgin forest, now less than a million hectares remains, and it seems certain that almost all of this will be gone by early in the next century.

The logging industry boomed in the 1960s and 1970s. Following his declaration of martial law in 1972, President Marcos handed out concessions of huge tracts of land to his cronies and senior military officials. Pressured to make payments on the foreign debt, the government encouraged log exports to the voracious Japanese market. Numerous companies were set up with exclusive opportunities to exploit forest resources and they rarely undertook reforestation.

This situation had some notable environmental consequences. Across the Philippines, especially on the island of Luzon, deforestation has led to greatly increased erosion and a drop in the land's ability to retain water during rainy periods. The resulting flash floods have destroyed bridges and roads. Silt washed off hillsides has filled reservoirs and channels. There are indications that this will seriously affect agricultural production. One study suggests that about 36,000 hectares of low lying farmland on the island of Palawan will need irrigation by the year 2005; but the hydrological effect of decreased forest cover will – in actuality – permit only about half of this land to be irrigated.[23]

Deforestation has many other effects. For example, about 20% of the poorest households in the Philippines use wood as a principal fuel for cooking and heating. As forests are destroyed, this wood becomes scarcer and more expensive and it absorbs an increasing share of the household budget.

With the growth rate of about 2.7% the Philippine population is expanding more rapidly than any other in East Asia. This growth, combined with the dropping productivity of the land and the displacement of traditional farmers by large-scale cash cropping for the export market has swelled the number of landless agricultural labourers. It has also encouraged a widespread migration of poor peasants from lowlands to the forested and highly erodible uplands.

It is in these peripheral areas largely beyond the effective control of the central government that civil dissent is rampant. Although the country has suffered from serious internal strife for decades, there are strong reasons to believe that resource depletion, stress and environmental degradation are increasingly powerful forces driving local discontent. This discontent is the basis of revolutionary movements. G. Hawes[24] has shown how the National Democratic Front (NDP) and the New People's

Army (NPA) have mobilized displaced and impoverished peoples into an ongoing insurgency. Cadres of these groups provide policing services within villages; they help the peasants define their situation and focus their discontent; and they assist the peasants in extracting concessions from landlords. A.G. Forter and D. Ganapin write:

> Agricultural labourers, marginalized tenants, and upland farmers, who are not only desperately poor but also lack a stable niche in the socio-economic system, constitute the main social base of support for the New People's Army . . . Given that these (poor) will continue to be the most rapidly growing social strata in the next two decades, the potential for violent protest is likely to grow rather than decline unless the relationship between population and agricultural land can be altered."[25]

Counterinsurgency

A most conspicuous contribution to global violence since 1945 has been American counterinsurgency warfare. The U.S. funded a thirty-year war in southeast Asia. It has supported repressive governments in the Third World against revolutionary forces. In fact, counterinsurgency has become a pillar of American global policy. Books have been written on how to conduct it.[26]

Counterinsurgency has amounted to the defence of the rich, powerful, and ruthless when they are challenged by the destitute and the desperate. Moral indignation has often moved people to sympathize wholeheartedly with the insurgents. However, a victory of the insurgents at times replaces one repressive regime by another. In the course of a power struggle, especially against a brutal regime and their ruthless sponsors, the insurgent leadership demands enormous sacrifices from its followers on whom it imposes harsh discipline. Having achieved victory, it often demands the same unquestioned obedience from the "liberated" population. This happened in Vietnam. In Cambodia the fanatical leadership of the Khmer Rouge unleashed genocidal fury against the helpless population. In both countries insurgency was a response to the introduction of tyrannical puppet regimes by the United States.

The trend toward authoritarian rule by the Sandinista regime, which initially was assumed to be building a people-oriented democracy, can also be attributed to intervention in the form of a vicious ten-year war against the people of Nicaragua waged by the Contras armed and sponsored by the U.S. At this time we cannot foretell what a victory of the insurgents in El Salvador, the Philippines, Ethiopia, Palestine, or Afghanistan will bring. It is clear, however, that chronic insurgency, for the most part triggered and/or sustained by intervention, is unlikely to lead to a just world order.

The Role of the Third World Elites

The gap between the interests of Third World elites and the needs of the Third World oppressed continues to be a principal source of chronic violence. Elites everywhere are concerned with maintaining wealth and privilege through domination of the power structure, but the compulsion must be especially strong when there is no comfortable middle class into which the elite can "parachute" if they lose their privileged position. The wide gap between the elites and the impoverished creates a compulsion to cling to power. Thus the revolutionary leader of yesterday becomes the tyrant of today. Brutal oppression creates constant danger of violent revolts and recurrent bloody struggles for power.

Another source of danger is the susceptibility of Third World leaders to military adventurism. This emergent phenomenon was conspicuous in the expansionist thrust of Libya into Sudan and more dramatically of Iraq into Kuwait. Military adventurism is typically associated with demagogy, for which poverty is a fertile soil. The poor equipped with weapons and often whipped into hysteria can take out their frustrations on scapegoats in massive indiscriminate violence. The leaders of the Third World who assume a military posture emulate the dictators of the 1930s. The oppressed eagerly seize the opportunity to vent their rage on clearly designated enemies both external and internal.

The Threat is Universal

The fact that chronic violence, whether in the form of interventions or interstate wars among the newly militarized Third World nations (e.g., Iran-Iraq), or in the form of tribal warfare punctuated by coups and massacres, is largely confined to the Third World should not blind us to the global danger inherent in it. With the end of superpower confrontation it appears possible to put the abolition of war as an institution on the agenda of world politics. However, as long as organized violence continues unabated anywhere, the war system is nurtured. Arms trading continues to be profitable and all the more difficult to eradicate. Intervention can be undertaken for reasons other than Cold War geopolitics, for instance, to insure access to or control of vital resources. As long as chronic warfare continues even "far away," all of us are threatened. This is why chronic violence should be regarded as one of the three cardinal threats to the human race.

The demise of the Cold War has given an impetus to peace. The momentum of this impetus can be sustained by a policy of promoting conflict resolution in the Third World, where violent conflicts go on unabated. Such a policy would entail rejection of war as an option by the affluent world and integration of the Third World into the global community as equal partners. A necessary concomitant of this process is a programme of building social and environmental justice, elimination of exploitation of poor countries by the rich.

It is in this process that middle powers, Canada perhaps foremost among them, can play a leading, creative role.

V.   RELATIONS WITH THE UNITED STATES

The frequently mentioned "special relationship" between the United States and Canada affects every aspect of Canadian life and every aspect of Canadian politics, foreign and domestic.

The United States is Canada's only neighbour. The border between the two states has been unfortified for well over a century, and the two wars between them (attempted invasions by Americans during the Revolutionary War and the War of 1812) belong to a forgotten age. The two countries are each other's principal trading partners. Culturally and ideologically they are closer than any other two sovereign states. That is to say, a citizen of one feels more at home in the other than in any other country. The relationship might be pointed out as an example to any other pair of contiguous states.

That strong interdependence is part of the relationship goes without saying. Moreover, because of disparate size, wealth, and power, the junior position of Canada in this relationship is also natural. However, the degree of this one-way dependence should be of concern to Canadians because of the addiction (the use of this term is justified above) of the United States to a militarized economy and a militarized foreign policy. Many Canadians are concerned about the persistent attempts on the part of Americans to establish and maintain hemispheric hegemony. They are also concerned about the indifference of recent American administrations to social welfare, which, in view of increasing economic dependence on the United States, may spread to Canada.

Military Arrangements

On August 17, 1940, Mackenzie King and Franklin D. Roosevelt met in a railway car and reaffirmed their commitment to the joint defence of North America. In marking the 50th anniversary of this event Murray Campbell wrote: " . . . the declaration demonstrated a clear awareness that the United States is obliged to defend Canada even if Canada does not wish to be defended."[27)]

Since 1959, the Defence and Development Production Sharing Arrangements (DDPSA) between Canada and the United States have created a North American common market in military production. Under the DDPSA the United States designs and builds the major weapons systems while Canada is given the opportunity to supply components through "offset" contracts. Essentially this is free trade in military commodities, with the important stipulation that this trade be kept in rough balance over the long term. The DDPSA and the "rough balance" clause have important economic and political consequences for Canada.

By far the greater part of Canadian military commodities are sold to the United States, making Canadian military industries dependent on obtaining U.S. military contracts. However, for every dollar made by Canadian companies selling military components to the U.S., the Canadian government must purchase from the U.S. weapons systems of an equal value. There is thus no possibility of Canada earning a balance of payment surplus with the result that there can be no long-term economic gain for Canada.

Since Canadian industries are building on U.S. design, Canadian production depends on imported subcomponents and tools. This means that every dollar of Canadian military exports generates a dollar of military imports, plus up to 20 cents worth of secondary imports. The result is a net trade deficit for Canada.

The same is true in the case of jobs. For every job that is created through military exports, another is lost by virtue of imports, because a major part of Canada's capital defence budget is spent in the United States. Canadian defence spending creates jobs in the United States, but not in Canada. Exports arranged through the DDPSA only compensate for this job loss; they do not create additional jobs in Canada in the way that civilian exports do.[28]

Canada's military production arrangements under the DDPSA are frequently justified by allegations of technological spinoffs for Canadian industries. However, because Canada's military industry has been developed as an addendum to that of the United States, the transfer of specialized military technology to civilian uses is rare or non-existent. As the head of one Canadian industry put it, "The things available to Canadian industry are not generally worth going after or are not at the leading edge of technology."[29] Moreover, the special "offset" arrangement negotiated to give Canadian companies a part of the work generated by the Department of National Defence's capital purchases leave even our military industries technologically impoverished. "Canada gets only the scraps" is the way the head of a leading military export firm put it. The failure of "offset contracts" to win technology benefits for Canada is confirmed in a survey by Aviation Week and Space Technology.[30]

In addition, Canada's access to "offset contracts" under the DDPSA has other costs. For example, the proviso that the industrial "benefits" of offsets be spread across the country (even though most of the expertise is in Ontario and Quebec) means that the focus is on alleged economic advantages rather than on a careful analysis of Canadian security needs.[31]

A further cost is that our present military production arrangements depend on our government's continued ability to purchase weapons systems from the United States. During the years 1982-1987, Canadian military spending increased 6 percent each year. During the fiscal year 1989-1990, the Department of National Defence still received $91 million more than the previous year despite government promises of budget cuts. Indeed, of seven government spending areas, defence was the only one to receive more money in 1989-1990. On the other hand, Canada's official aid to developing countries, which represents only 3 percent of federal spending, was made to shoulder 23 percent of government spending cuts in 1989-1990. A further cut of $558 million in addition to the 1.8 billion announced in 1989 means that over six years aid to developing countries will be cut by $2.36 billion, plummeting to less than 0.43 percent of our GNP.

Canada's military production arrangements have other economic costs. Under the Defence Industry Productivity Programmes (DIPP), the federal government grants public subsidies of about $200 million annually to enable industries – many of which are subsidiaries of U.S. military contractors – to develop and produce military commodities for export to the U.S. military. The result has been the creation of a Canadian military industry primed with public subsidies to meet production requirements set in the U.S. to suit American policies.

The primary aim of the DIPP programme is economic development. Yet studies both in the United States and in Canada have clearly demonstrated that investment in military industries is a poor means of job creation. For example, a recent study by the Canadian Union of Public Employees shows that in 1983-1984 National Defence spending on goods and services created 22,000 jobs, while consumer spending created 39,000 jobs. In the light of this, it is estimated that the $54 billion that the Canadian government plans to spend on military procurement over the years 1989-2000 could cost the country 918,000 jobs.[33] Thus the DIPP programme actually contributes to unemployment by supporting increasingly complex and specialized military technologies at the expense of the development and production of civilian ones that would result in more jobs for Canadians.

The United States Defence Department will not guarantee extension of contracts for military commodities beyond the initial order. If the product requires financial aid from the Canadian government and (as is likely) has no market in Canada, an additional cost of the DIPP programme is generated. Consequently, it is the Canadian tax payer who takes the risk through the DIPP programme funding for capital costs related to certain export contracts.[34]

However, probably the greatest long-term cost of the DIPP programme is that individual Canadian firms are encouraged to become more dependent on military production for export. Once created, this dependence becomes a force for sustaining and expanding Canadian participation in the international arms race.

In addition to the economic costs of Canada's military production arrangements, there are important and far-reaching political costs as well. Again, these flow from the fact that the survival of Canadian military production depends fully on the United States.

While the U.S. Congress tends to view Canadian production of U.S. military commodities as the loss of American jobs, the Administration supports these arrangements, viewing them as indicative of Canada's support for and cooperation in a single continental defence policy. If Canada should withdraw this cooperation – for example, by refusing to permit the testing of cruise missiles on Canadian territory – the U.S. administration would soon cease to protect Canadian military industrial interests in the United States and there would be serious consequences for Canada. Plants would close. Canadian engineers would leave in large numbers for the United States, and there would be major unemployment, especially in Ontario and Quebec, where our military-related industries are concentrated.

In sum, Canada has developed a stake in maintaining current U.S. perception. Canada has given the United States a direct lever to influence Canada's military procurement decisions, its defence policy, and even foreign policy decisions.

Because our current military production arrangements under the DDPSA require Canada to purchase major weapons systems from the United States, Canada has given up much of its freedom to make independent military procurement decisions. Thus our purchases of major military equipment cannot be a careful response to our own defence needs. Moreover, in giving a foreign power direct influence, if not control, over important decisions on military equipment, Canada is to some extent giving that power the means to influence our very view of the world. Because weapons systems come with built-in strategies, roles, and assumptions about threat, the Canadian defence establishment has come to accept uncritically both the U.S. perception of a world dominated by East-West rivalries and the U.S. perception of how to deal with international conflict.[35]

This is clearly indicated in the 1987 Canadian Defence *White Paper* (which at the time of writing is still Canada's stated defence policy). The White Paper views war between heavily nuclear-armed nations as thinkable. The language contains phrases such as "should deterrence fail," "if hostilities were to occur," etc., key ideas of the U.S. defence policy of the Reagan era. However, the burgeoning of the world-wide peace movement of the 1980s clearly indicates the public's opposition to the idea that a nuclear war can be fought and won.

Moreover, the defence *White Paper* of 1987 views a Soviet Nuclear attack on North America as the greatest threat to Canada. This is contrary to the opinion of most Canadians, according to polls conducted by the Canadian Institute for International Peace and Security in 1987 and 1989. In 1987, CIIPS found that most Canadians saw the arms race as the greatest threat to their security, while in 1989 CIIPS found that most Canadians view nuclear proliferation, global pollution, international crime, and the spread of disease the greatest threats to their security.[36]

The influence of the U.S. military policy on the 1987 Canadian defence *White Paper* clearly demonstrates that Canadian independence in formulating defence policy has become a casualty of the military production arrangements with the United States. As Project Ploughshares Research Director Ernie Regehr points out, "To the extent that national sovereignty and independence can be measured by a capacity to deploy national defence forces, decide when and how the defence forces are to be mobilized, and produce the equipment those forces need, Canada must be judged to have forfeited a considerable measure to both independence and sovereignty."[37]

This loss of independence has led to glaring inconsistencies between Canada's foreign and defence policies. Despite Canada's foreign policy statement in support of "global security at progressively lower levels of weapons, both nuclear and conventional,"[38] Canada is allowing testing of the second generation of the destabilizing cruise missiles; it is promoting the use of Canadian air-space for U.S. low-level fighter and bomber exercises that threaten to undo whatever arms-control progress has been made; it is providing facilities for American anti-submarine warfare exercises in Nanoose Bay and Jarvis Inlet; and it is acquiescing in the increasing militarization of the Canadian Arctic. Also while claiming to be a non-nuclear weapons state, Canada currently places no restrictions on the production of components for nuclear weapons systems such as the Trident submarine, and the MX and cruise missiles. Instead of acting on the basis of broad public support for Canadian initiatives to promote international peace and security, our government is caught up in the elements of "maintaining and managing America's global conflict with the Soviet Union."[39]

It is clear that the current approach to military production in Canada undermines constructive Canadian policies for peace and justice. As John M. Treddenick, an economist at the Royal Military College of Canada warns, "The danger is that neither Canada's security interests nor its economic interests will be effectively addressed. But more importantly, the intermingling of military and economic considerations may blunt the nation's sensitivity to the dangers of the arms race with the result that incentives to search for ways to reduce armament expenditures may be submerged."[40]

It is quite apparent that Canada's current military production arrangements come with considerable cost attached. This cost could be increased under the Free Trade Agreement which failed to guarantee or expand Canada's access to the U.S. military market. In the face of increased U.S. protectionism, the Free Trade Agreement may increase the political price to Canada of maintaining this access by requiring increased cooperation in testing U.S. weapons systems and increased purchase of U.S. military hardware. For example, a U.S. request to use Canadian territory for testing or even deploying Star Wars components is a distinct possibility.

Economic Arrangements: The Free Trade Agreement

Ordinarily free trade agreements between nations stimulate expansion of trade and confer economic advantages on both. In the case of the free trade agreement between Canada and the United States, several of the consequences have been detrimental to Canada. The reasons for this are to be found in the economic dominance of the United States over Canada, which permits the United States to impose its economic policies on Canada.

One of the most immediate consequences of the free trade agreement has been loss of jobs in Canada. The Canadian Labour Council estimates the number of jobs lost to date (first half of 1990) at 70,000. The number is still increasing. The losses have affected fish processing, agriculture, manufacturing, retail trade. In fact hardly any sector of the Canadian economy has been spared.

American labour practices have been less favourable to labour than Canadian. In particular, American labour is less unionized. The free trade agreement generates pressure on labour by the employers, facilitating de-unionization and depression of wages.

The effects on Canadian industry are equally damaging. Five American states have set up offices in Canada to help companies move south. Companies that have moved or closed include Inglis, Burlington Carpet, Rowntree, Litton, Northern Telecon, Dominion Textile, Unisys, Sivace, Picker International, Skylar

Peppler, Sterling Drug, Midas Muffler, Fiberglass Canada – the tally is in the hundreds and continues to grow.

The predominant social philosophy of the United States, which Herbert Hoover once identified as "rugged individualism" (a term of approval) looks askance at social programmes. The effect of the Free Trade Agreement has been the undermining of Canada's social programming. Provincial transfer payments (which fund health and education) have been cut. There have been major changes in unemployment insurance to make it resemble more closely the less than adequate American insurance. Old age security and family allowances have been reduced. The changes detrimental to social programmes are indirect effects of the Free Trade Agreement, since the agreement is a step toward completing the economic *Anschluss* of Canada to the United States and so creates a political climate favourable to adopting American economic practices.

The highly unpopular 7 percent Goods and Services Tax is intended to make up for the decline of tariff revenue resulting from the Free Trade Agreement. The cuts in special programmes are likewise related to the loss of tariff revenues.

In sum, the Free Trade Agreement is another step in the direction of subordinating Canada to the U.S., more precisely, the U.S. business interests, not known to be concerned with the welfare of their own population and surely less with the welfare of Canadians.

Prospects of a Firmer Basis for Canadian-American Friendship

Our emphasis on the dangers inherent in the domination by the U.S. over Canadian security and economic policies should not detract from the potential of the long standing Canadian-American friendship. If immense changes in political climate are realized in the Soviet Union in a matter of a few years and in Eastern Europe in a matter of months (or weeks or days), there is reason to hope that changes of comparable import can occur in the United States.

Canadians should be alert to any incipient changes presaging emancipation from the present hang-ups. We should be ready to give enthusiastic moral support to all harbingers of such emancipation.

Voices are being raised in the U.S. that could not be heard a year ago. What is surprising is not what is being said (these things were said repeatedly throughout the last four decades) but who says them. In this instance we cite a pamphlet by Larry Agran, Mayor of Irvine, California. Irvine is a major town in Orange County, traditionally the stronghold of right wing politics and intense dedication to the defence industry very largely concentrated in this region:

As Mayor of a militarily dependent community, I ask the citizens who elected me to look beyond our share of the $3 billion in prime military contracts that come to Orange County each year. I ask them to consider the choice. 'What's more important for America and for the world,' I ask, 'maintaining a Rapid Deployment Force of doubtful military value or building rapid transit systems and other energy-efficient transportation improvements that will allow us to overcome our worst-in-the-nation traffic problems while reducing our demand for fossil fuels?'

What is more important? Producing more nerve gas, more weapons grade plutonium and more hydrogen bombs – at a cost of more than $10 billion per year? Or reforesting the Earth at half the annual cost?

What is more important? Pouring $5 billion per year into Star Wars research? Or using that same amount of money to provide comprehensive family planning services, not just in America but world-wide?

These are not abstract questions of choice. What's at stake here is nothing less than the moral basis for governments in the late 20th century. A generation ago Dr. Martin Luther King, Jr. put it this way: 'A nation that continues year after year to spend more on nuclear defence than on programs of social uplift is approaching spiritual death.' Dr. King understood that Americans had to make a moral choice because America was – and is – in moral crisis. The moral crisis we face – a continuing militarism that destroys us spiritually just as it bankrupts us financially – is a crisis every bit as acute as the tyranny that caused the American Independence Movement in the 18th century, or the enslavement of African Americans that caused the abolitionist movement in the 19th century, or the outrage of segregation that caused the Civil Rights movement in the 20th century.

The moral crisis of militarism cannot be resolved by compromise any more than colonialism, slavery, and segregation were susceptible to compromise. We cannot compromise with the Cold Warriors who still hold the Republican Party in their grip. Nor can we compromise with the Congressional Democrats – many of them self-described liberals who say they agree with our goals but who counsel caution in cutting the Pentagon budget for fear that the Democratic Party be perceived as 'weak on defence.' Never mind that a Democratic Party still endorsing Cold War military budgets is weak on urban policy, weak on education, weak on health, weak on environmental protection; it's just plain weak on everything that counts.

We must reject suggestions from any quarter that we be content with a 'leveling off' of the military budget at $300 billion per year or perhaps achieving a $1 billion or $2 billion cut here or there. This is what Dr. King called the 'tranquilizing drug of gradualism' – and we should have none of it.[41]

A year or two ago talk of this sort would surely spell the political death of any elected official. There is no guarantee that this will not happen to Mayor Agran. But the fact that he dares put his political life on the line in the cause of sanity speaks volumes about the change of political winds. We believe that some prominent spokesmen of Canadian government can match this courage. Eventually Canadian-American friendship will be solidly based on common devotion to genuine peace, genuine security, and global justice.

The liberation of Canadian-American friendship from the imperatives of the Soviet-American power struggle depends on the cementing of Soviet-American friendship. Although by no means inevitable, this partnership is certainly possible. Further, we believe that a definitive resolution of superpower conflict would be a key to productive and lasting cooperation between all of the highly industrialized, economically powerful nations. Such cooperation, in turn, could be a key to global integration, only, however, provided a just global order is a principal aim of this cooperation. This would require a change of direction, which, although possible, is by no means inevitable. The pattern of economic colonialization, precluding sustainable development, may well persist, in which case the hope for world peace, kindled by the demise of the East-West ideological confrontation, will be dashed.

VI. RELATIONS WITH THE THIRD WORLD

The relationship between Canada and the Third World has three principal components: trade, investment, and aid.

Trade

The economic well being of a country depends in large measure on its ability to trade with other countries – the exchange of its surpluses for its deficiencies. Opportunity to trade is thus a necessary condition for the economic well being of a country. It is, however, by no means a sufficient one. Whether foreign trade benefits a country depends on the terms of trade. These may be advantageous to one side but disadvantageous to the other.

In examining Canada's trade relations with non-oil producing countries of the Third World, we find that Canada consistently comes out ahead, partly because Canada, like other developed countries, restricts imports from the Third World and partly because the prices of commodities exported by the Third World countries have fallen. During the 1960s and 1970s these prices have fallen by 40% relative to the prices of imports from developed countries. In effect the trade in commodities amounts to transfer of income from underdeveloped to developed countries. The United Nations Conference on Trade and Development (UNCTAD) has estimated this transfer to be about $17 billion per year. To put it in concrete terms, in 1972 a country like Tanzania could buy a tractor for five tonnes of tea; in 1979 the same tractor cost 13 tonnes of tea.[42]

Import restrictions produce a similar imbalance. Again taking Tanzania as an example, sales to Canada of jute bale twine made in that country have been declining because of restrictions aimed at protecting small Canadian producers of synthetic twine, even though the biodegradable jute is preferred by Canadian farmers.[43]

The Bangladesh jute minister was quoted as saying that his country would rather see Canadian tariff restrictions against jute lifted than receive $4 million worth of direct aid.[44]

To put it in a nutshell, Canada sells more to the Third World than it buys. So in a way the Third World can be regarded as giving Canada aid through trade rather than vice versa. If Canada is to be a socially responsible trading partner, we must actively pursue an even balance of trade with each of our Third World partners.

In order to counteract the most destructive effects of competition between poor countries for trade with us, we should institute preferential treatment for countries with relatively progressive policies on workers' rights and the environment. This would also help to protect Canadian workers from competition with exploited workers abroad. Countries striving to improve their workers' position would have easier access to our markets, while countries which prevent improvements in labour relations would lose an unfair competitive advantage. Such selection of trade partners (rather than reliance on across the board trade-inhibiting tariffs) would ultimately benefit both sides. Similarly, such a policy could also be made to promote environmental responsibility while protecting our economy from attempts to gain a competitive advantage at the expense of the environment.

Investment

Looking at the investment component, we see that the Third World also confers advantages on Canada by hosting private investments. These have been steadily increasing. By 1976 Canadian investors had placed more investment dollars in the Third World than in industrialized countries. Part of the profits are remitted to Canada in the form of dividends and interest payments. Another part, between 24% and 50% is reinvested abroad, expanding the stock of Canadian-owned foreign investments. This process is part of the global economy, whose principal actors are transnational corporations.

Transnationals rationalize their existence by claiming to maximize efficiency, to facilitate transfer of technologies, and to promote industrial development in the developing countries. Their primary goal is to increase their profit margin, which they do by locating their branch plants and subsidiaries in regions where they have easy access to cheap raw materials, where labour is abundant and wages are low, where there are few corporate responsibilities demanded of them, and where ecological standards are lax or non-existent. In addition, the host country, desirous of attracting foreign investments, frequently grants them concessions in the form of tax breaks.

Intrafirm trade enables transnationals to gain benefits from currency fluctuations and to minimize their world-wide tax, through a process known as transfer pricing. The parent company and subsidiaries or two subsidiaries trade with each other in such a manner as to show low profits in countries where the taxation is high and higher profits in countries where the taxation rate is low. Thus they minimize total tax. In this way transnationals provide a mechanism whereby their weight in the world economy increases.

Transnationals are in large measure responsible for the worst impact of development on poor countries. Even though populations in the Third World countries have greatly increased, vast areas of their good agricultural land, instead of providing basic food requirements, is put to cash crops such as coffee, cotton, bananas, flowers, or drug ingredients. In other words, more land in the poorer countries is used to provide for the needs or wants of the richer countries than when the poor countries were under imperial rule. In this way, the break-up of the colonial system, instead of improving the life of the erstwhile subjugated peoples worsened their lot by paving the way for profit-oriented rather than people-oriented development.

The Commission on Transnational Corporations May 1978 Economic and Social Council record stated:

The importance of the role of transnational corporations in developing countries may be judged by the fact . . . that the majority of the developing countries' imports, in particular of intermediate and capital goods originate with such corporations, while a large proportion of these countries' exports pass directly or indirectly through them . . . [45]

Many developing countries, therefore, have little control over their own resources. Eighty to ninety percent of the trade in tea, coffee, cocoa, cotton, forest products, tobacco, jute, copper, iron ore, and bauxite is controlled in the case of each commodity by the three to six largest transnationals.[46] This enriches the local powerful land owners and the transnationals that own the land, but leaves the peasants landless and destitute. It creates shortages of food, driving prices high, and it explains to a degree the hunger prevalent in many regions of the Third World.

Since the earnings of subsidiaries are high because of low costs of production, decapitalization occurs. This means that over a period of time profits in terms of interest and dividends earned by the subsidiaries exceed the initial investments made by the parent company. This impoverishes Third World countries and partly explains why after years of investment by great economic owners, the vast majority of the people are no better off.

If there is any section of a poor country's society that derives any benefits from the subsidiaries located on their soil, it is the few industrialists, the land owners, the upper middle class, and the military. The transnationals, by providing very lucrative positions to a few nationals of the host country, and by allowing a percentage of shares to be held by them, create vested interest among the elites of Third World countries in hosting investments. Since it is invariably these elites that wield political influence and power, the transnationals are assured of a favourable and secure environment.

It must be understood that the transnationals could never make such inroads without the support of the local economic elites, who exploit their poor and collaborate with the transnationals in allowing their poor people and their resources to be further exploited.   Such an unjust order often cannot be maintained .without a dictatorship and strong military presence. Fearful of uprisings, underdeveloped countries become client states and are bestowed generously with arms.

The role of the transnationals in obstructing people-oriented development in the Third World should be addressed by Canadian policy. Subsidies and taxes are a potentially significant "carrot-and-stick" tool for government to influence the behaviour of the private sector of the economy. A company operating in Canada should be evaluated on the basis of its employment practices, environmental impact, use of national resources, and involvement with the arms race. A company should be held responsible for the actions of its parent and subsidiary companies world wide. Comparisons with other companies in the same business would be the basis of preferential subsidy and tax treatment.

The International Monetary Fund.

Interdependence is a fact of modern life, and world problems require global bodies which can cooperatively put the world's resources to work to solve the problems. The International Monetary Fund is a potentially valuable instrument to stimulate investment in Third World development. The decision-making structure within the IMF is weighted among states by financial strength. This makes Canada's potential as a reformist force considerable. This force could be used to bring the performance of the IMF in accord with its stated goal – to promote sustainable development in the underdeveloped countries.

For the most part, these goals are not being served. The investment coordinated by the IMF has led to chronic indebtedness and periodic crises. Equality of opportunity among the world's people is farther off and more elusive than ever. The IMF's claim to be non-political is unjustified. The conditions which are the prerequisites to most government and private development loans have distinctly political significance. Some of the measures required to be implemented in a country applying for a development loan are supposed to reduce inflation in that country. Such measures involve cutting government employment and public services. Balance of payments of loan recipients is supposed to be improved through support for export production at the expense of production for domestic needs.

While these policies are economically justified, they are not necessarily consistent with other political goals – those related to people-oriented sustainable development. On the contrary, the policies imposed on loan recipients as conditions for qualifying for loans have so far been counterproductive. They create more serious problems than they solve. For instance they tend to produce heavy unemployment. Ironically, instead of reducing inflation, they effectively aggravate it in real domestic terms (relation of prices to wages), producing hunger and homelessness. These are, of course, unacceptable evils in themselves, but their effect is magnified by the usual government responses to the resulting popular unrest. A government in such a situation is faced with the options of relaxing the severity of the austerity measures, maintaining power and "order" through destructive and expensive repression, or giving up power. Each of these options prevents the imposed measures from achieving their intended purpose. In a fundamentally capitalist world it is inevitable that international economic institutions impose conditions for credit designed to protect the interests of creditors. But these conditions should address the causes of poverty with a view to supporting the most realistic progressive efforts to achieve people-oriented sustainable development.

Economic development that does not meet human needs is more accurately termed exploitation. The most obvious human needs include food, water, clothing, shelter, health care, communication, education, and employment. Investment in these needs, if undertaken consistently, yields economically measurable results in productivity.

Human development is resisted by privileged groups in poor countries because it is a threat to their position. That is why the international community must insist on control of capital to insure encouragement of democratization. Such insistence necessarily entails challenging the complicity of affluent countries in continuing the exploitation of the impoverished populations to serve their own interests. Canada can contribute to this process very significantly by taking positions in favour of human development in the IMF and in the World Bank.

Aid

A conspicuous form of direct aid is transfer of food – the most important form of direct aid. An essential component of long-term development programmes is the elimination of starvation, the most dramatic and acute form of degradation of human resources.

Though the First World has become accustomed to the slaughter of civilians in wars and insurrections, it has fortunately become sensitized to starvation. Perhaps this is because when starvation hit closer to home, it received more publicity. When 20 million people died of hunger in India during the last three decades of the nineteenth century, few people in the West were even aware of these deaths. But when the Allied forces liberated the Nazi concentration camp victims at the end of World War II, they were shocked by the sight of living skeletons, victims of deliberately imposed starvation.[47] More recently, television has brought the spectacle of famine into the daily lives of North Americans and Europeans.

Food has been a primary response of western countries to the plight of the Third World. Fully one fifth of all the aid provided by the Canadian International Development Agency (CIDA) and its predecessors has been in the form of food.

Famine is not always the result of catastrophes. It is made more likely by the neglect of sustainable agriculture. This neglect is in some ways encouraged by food aid which is not part of a realistic plan for agricultural self-sufficiency.

Food aid may lower agricultural prices, resulting in switches to profitable cash crops. It may enable a government to avoid forming a policy to achieve food sufficiency. Emergency food aid should, of course, be unconditional. But regular food aid should be made conditional on the implementation of a realistic programme to achieve self-sufficiency. This may necessitate such measures as land reform or fiscal discouragement of cash cropping. We could offer financial aid and professional support for such measures.

Long term food dependency is a serious and dangerous obstacle to development which Canada should avoid encouraging, while doing everything possible to respond to emergencies.

Drawing a balance, we must conclude that so far Canada's aid policy has failed to achieve what an aid programme is supposed to achieve, to pave the way for integrating the Third World into a global community. This means that an overhaul of the delivery system is insufficient. The aid policy needs to be changed. The changes must involve not only the type of aid offered, not merely a re-design of the aid package, but it must also involve the choice of aid partners.

There should be only one overall goal in giving aid to Third World countries, namely, to assist in people-oriented development. All other purposes – brightening the image of a generous giver, extending the sphere of influence of the donor country, extending the market for the donor's entrepreneurs – all of these interfere with a programme's effectiveness. Neither pure "altruism" nor conventionally conceived "national interest" should govern aid policy. Only enlightened self-interest should be the guide. Self-interest becomes enlightened when it is integrated with every one else's self-interest, that is, becomes collective self-interest.

The first step in the fundamental reform of aid policy should, therefore, be the separation of developmental and commercial objectives. To call exports "promotion", to call disposal of surplus food or public subsidization of private enterprise "aid" is sheer hypocrisy. In short:

(1)   Canada must put a stop to transferring its own economic problems on the Third World and calling it "aid". Specifically, the subsidizing of private companies investing in the Third World does not belong to CIDA.

(2)   Food aid is to a great extent counter-productive. It should be confined to well-planned efforts to relieve emergencies and unrelated to our own commercial interests.

Removing commercial interest from aid to the Third World is a prerequisite to making aid serve its single legitimate purpose, namely, to insure people-oriented sustainable development and then the ultimate integration of the developing countries into a just social order. In contrast, political content cannot be removed from aid, because authentic development is inherently a political process. Development is a means to an end, not an end in itself. The goal is, as has been repeatedly emphasized, the integration of humanity into a humane system and this system into a rich, viable biosphere. If this goal is not to remain a utopian ideal, it must be made a guideline of a political process.[48)]

Throughout the Cold War, CIDA continued to link aid to strategic ploys, to rationalize all programmes as tactical moves in the western campaign against enemy "isms." This approach defeats what should be Canada's purpose in providing development aid. It makes Canada appear as a purveyor of neo-colonialism and precludes an alliance with the supposed beneficiaries of aid, namely, the people of the Third World, instead of just their governments and elites. The politics that guide CIDA should be based on solidarity with oppressed people and their struggle for political and economic liberation. The following criteria should provide guidelines for a Canadian aid programme:

(1)   Bilateral aid should be reserved for countries with popularly supported governments, genuinely committed to

eradication of poverty at its roots and to accomplishing this in a self-reliant way.

(2)   Conversely, development assistance should not be given to the government of an underdeveloped country where gross social inequalities are maintained. Even if political considerations were entirely removed from aid programmes, i.e., even if aid were given on the basis of immediate humanitarian concerns, supplying countries with elitist and repressive regimes is unlikely to do much for the people of those countries.

(3)   A vital criterion in selecting aid partners should be the human rights record of the prospective partners. Human rights include not only political and civil rights but also economic, social, religious, and cultural rights. Whenever and wherever these are violated, underdevelopment occurs and will continue. This is because violations of these rights entail more than a violation of integrity of individuals and groups. They preclude individuals' and groups' participation in the collective effort of development, indispensable in authentic and sustainable development.

In sum, development entails not only the economy of a country but also the development of the population – cultural, political, and ideological.

In other words, the goals of giving aid (and therefore in selecting foreign governments as aid partners) should be not only satisfaction of "basic needs" (although this should be a prerequisite) but also of "basic rights" – the rights of participation. The right of participation means the right to belong. Belonging is the antithesis of alienation, the pervasive disease of humanity caught in lopsided development pressures.

The Swedish aid agency might serve as a model for CIDA. It is based on giving priority support to countries earnestly engaged in eradicating poverty. Admittedly, this could mean decreasing the amount of aid allocation in the short run, but not necessarily in the long run. The selection principle could amount to wielding a political clout. There is no reason why a political clout should not be wielded in the interest of people who are in desperate need of genuine assistance. As the basis of selection of aid partners becomes apparent, political changes in the right direction may be primed in the Third World. In this way expansion of aid would be justified.

Non-government Organizations

In some cases, where a government is not an appropriate partner in administering Canadian foreign aid, it may be possible to aid non-governmental organizations operating in the country. Organizations working to build small-scale cooperative enterprises, educational, health and similar programmes would be good candidates for support from Canada. In this connection, a word is in order on the role of Canadian NGO's in aid programmes. It is important for our NGO's to be able to help their counterparts in the Third World to combat the causes of poverty. In general, they deserve praise as effective, disinterested, grass-roots-oriented institutions dedicated to aid giving. However, this is not universally true, and Canadians who support NGO's through private donations might be advised to go through a short check list in deciding whether to give:

(1)   Is the NGO committed to combating the real causes of poverty and underdevelopment, not only in the recipient countries but also in Canada?

(2)   Does the NGO leave the decision-making control over supported projects in the hands of the local organization in the recipient countries and avoid fostering economic dependence?

(3)   Are the projects and organizations funded by the NGO assessing their own positions and objectives, specifically how they fit into the larger framework of society and how they relate to the overall goal of changing relationships in the direction of social justice?

(4)   Does the fund-raising appeal of the NGO accurately portray the causes of underdevelopment or does it distort them?

(5)   Is the standard of the NGO itself democratic? Is the organization accountable to its members and to the donor?[49]

Toward People-oriented Development

The key to a non-utopian, just global social order is sustainable, equitable, people-oriented development. The meanings of all these words are familiar, but in order to present our recommendations in a proper light, we will spell them out.

By "non-utopian" we mean realizable, not merely imaginable as an ideal. Therefore in discussing a non-utopian future it is not sufficient to describe it; it is also necessary to indicate how to get it or at least how to take a direction toward it.

By "sustainable" we mean a process that can go on, not merely get started. Every track runner knows that although in a spurt he/she can reach a speed in the neighbourhood of ten metres per second, he/she cannot keep it up. A people-oriented sustainable development is one that meets the needs of the present generation without compromising the ability of future generations to meet their own needs.

By a "just global social order" we mean one in which the tight interdependence of all the people on the planet is coupled with equal status of every one as a human being entitled to partake in the bounty of the planet and having some say in the way the affairs of humanity are run.

In general, development is a process that manifests itself in growth of some kind, particularly in growth of complexity. An organism develops as it matures. In particular, human beings, if they mature normally, grow mentally as well as physically. Under favourable circumstances, they also develop morally as they become socialized into cooperative relationships with other members of the community in which they live.

Our civilization has been marked by increasingly rapid development of technology. This rapid pace became noticeable only comparatively recently (on the historical scale), that is, about 200 years ago, at first primarily in Europe and in countries settled by Europeans. In the early stages this development conferred conspicuous advantages on at least a sector of the population and was generally perceived by its beneficiaries as a boon to humanity, since it brought emancipation from drudgery, longer life spans, greater comforts, etc.

At present we begin to see ever more clearly the dangers inherent in the uncontrolled burgeoning of technology. In the first instance, the cooperation of technology to feed the addiction to power (as in the development of genocidal weapons), in the depletion of resources, the degradation of the environment, and in the use of technology in covert exploitation of the impoverished by the affluent, for instance, by recruiting impoverished countries for the weapons market or by influencing the direction of their development for the benefit of the affluent and to the detriment of the supposed beneficiaries of development aid.

When it became clear that technology driven developments create more hazards and more misery than they alleviate, the concept of people-oriented development arose, not directed toward feeding power addiction, not wasting resources, not despoiling or degrading the environment, and, most important, a development that can be of benefit to all over a long time. Such a development would alleviate rather than aggravate the presently increasing polarization of humanity into the affluent and the destitute, which, as we have seen, obstructs collective global effort in coping with the paramount issues of our time: common security, environmental protection, equitable distribution of resources.

High on the agenda of people-oriented sustainable development is the goal of leaving an inhabitable planet to our children. Humans are probably the only animals aware of their mortality and worrying about it. Religions arose probably, at least in part, as ways of coping with the prospect of individual death. Of ways of coping, one is directly relevant to the ethics of development, namely, coming to terms with personal death by identifying with our children, who will live after us. Some of us may even feel that as long as we can hope to live in the memories of our children, we have in a way conquered personal death.

Protecting children is our privilege as mammals. Commitment to people-oriented development is, therefore, a recognition and appreciation of this privileged status in the scheme of life. The commitment is expressed in the United Nations Convention on the Rights of the Child.

The conditions for the realization of people-oriented development have been cogently summarized in a document generally known as the *Brundtland Report*. They are:

A political system that secures effective citizen participation in decision making;

An economic system that is able to generate surpluses and technical knowledge on a self-reliant and sustained basis;

A social system that provides for solutions for the tensions arising from disharmonious development;

A production system that respects the obligation to preserve the ecological basis for development.;

A technological system that fosters sustainable patterns of trade and finance;

An administrative system that is feasible and has the capacity for self-correction.[50]

In listing these conditions the intent was not to state them as pre-requisites that must be realized before people-oriented development can be implemented. Rather they are goals to be worked toward while people-oriented sustainable development is going on. They must reinforce each other.

Obstacles to realizing people-oriented development.

The economic foundation of the affluent world has been the so-called "free enterprise system." It is ideologically supported by a conviction that society is best served when individuals are left free to manage their own economic interests, use capital in the interest of private profit, unimpeded by government restrictions, and when the state keeps out of all economic activities, leaving market forces of demand and supply to regulate prices and wages. It is this freedom more than any of the other freedoms and rights that, according to this philosophy, constitutes a free society and defines democracy.

This conviction was most cogently expressed by Adam Smith in his classic treatise, *The Wealth of Nations*, the theoretical foundation of the free enterprise system. We read:

Every one, so long as he does not violate the laws of justice, is left perfectly free to pursue his own interest in his own way and to bring forth his industry and capital into competition with those of every other man or order of men.[51]

Here is the philosophy of individualism in a nutshell. It carried a tremendous appeal to the industrious and gifted people who rode the crest of the Industrial Revolution. And, as is usual, the appealing social philosophy provided its own ethos, also cogently stated by Adam Smith:

It is not from the benevolence of the butcher, the brewer, and the baker, that we expect our dinner, but from their regard to their own interest. We address ourselves not to their humanity but to their self-love and never talk to them of our own necessities but of their advantages. Nobody but a beggar chooses to depend chiefly on the benevolence of his fellow citizens.[52]

From this ethically justified selfishness of individuals, collective benefits were supposed to arise through the operation of the market. Adam Smith compared the dynamics of the market to an "invisible hand" that produces these benefits. Not the decree of some benevolent potentate but something analogous to a natural law increases the well-being of a population if only the law is allowed to operate without interference.

This is the way the capitalist system was supposed to work. But it does not. Along with economic power, the enterpreneurial class has acquired formidable political power which has been used to assure the benefits conferred by profits and to relieve the entrepreneurs from the obligations that originally accompanied those benefits, namely, the obligations to accept the hazards of competitive free enterprise.

Throughout the Cold War, the superpowers attempted to export their respective economic systems and their attendant ideologies to the countries of the Third World. Whether they believed that choosing the one or the other path would benefit the people of those countries is not relevant. The "proselytising" attempts were primarily components of a strategy to bring the countries into the one or the other sphere and to keep them there.

If we are concerned with helping the countries of the Third World follow the path of people-oriented development, we should carefully assess the appropriateness of the different economic systems for achieving this goal.

The free enterprise system was most successful in improving the lives of most people in what is called the West. Three circumstances must be kept in mind in assessing the potential of that system elsewhere and in a different era. First, the development driven by the free enterprise system depended to a great extent on the existence of what has come to be called the Middle Class. This class comprises people who are engaged in productive work (rather than living by exploiting other people's labour like, say, a land-owning aristocracy) but not crushed by debilitating drudgery. Hence they can dispose of some creative energy and constitute a market for domestic production. In the period of the most rapid development of free enterprise, the middle class comprised merchants, free artisans, and professionals, as well as entrepreneurs who participated actively in the organization and management of enterprises. Second, the development of the free enterprise system took place at a time when ecological problems were not nearly so severe as they have become in the last decades. Third, the development took place before export of war technology became a major means of exploitation of the peoples of the Third World.

The situation in the Third World today is quite different. There are several reasons why unhampered free enterprise cannot achieve the sort of development that constituted "progress" in the West. First, the middle class in most Third World countries is numerically small and a large portion of it consists of government employees rather than self-reliant small entrepreneurs or members of free professions with a stake in general well-being. Second, the severe ecological problems, unknown in the early stages of the Industrial Revolution, cannot be solved unless development is appropriately guided. Such guidance is incompatible with free-wheeling private enterprise. Finally, absence of control leaves a poor country vulnerable to the new vicious form of exploitation: arms trade, the latter-day version of the opium trade foisted on China in the 19th century. The recipients of sophisticated weapons (the governments of underdeveloped countries) are usually seduced by fear of their neighbours (who are similarly seduced) or by power addiction (occasionally bursting out in overt aggression) or by the need to preserve dominance over their own populations. Uninhibited free enterprise on the global scale precludes effective restriction of the arms trade, a prerequisite of people-oriented development of poor countries.

On the other hand, the dramatic failure of command economies in countries where they were adopted should forewarn against this type of economic system. The recommendation of the *Brundtland Report* – "an economic system able to generate surpluses and technical knowledge on a self-reliant and sustained basis," seems reasonable and promising but represents a goal rather than a plan. Clearly, recommendations concerning specific economic systems to be encouraged in the Third World should be guided by pragmatic rather than ideological considerations.

Meeting a population's survival needs is an essential precondition of any human development. When these needs are met, a middle class can be created by opening up educational and enterpreneurial opportunities, by protecting and encouraging democratic institutions, by recognizing collective labour rights, and, above all, by encouraging participation of people in the management of their affairs, which, more than anything else, induces a determination to improve one's lot and thus to take advantage of educational and entrepreneurial opportunities. Free enterprise policies may well play a substantial part in this development. On the other hand, inculcating habits of cooperation, a sense of belonging (related to the feeling that one's condition matters to others and to the society at large) characterize the ideals of socialism. These ideals and many practices designed to serve them have been incorporated in many countries of the West where free enterprise, although at times guided and controlled, has by no means been abolished. Canada is one of them. The true essence of socialism is neither government monopoly nor a dictatorship of a class but integration of society into cooperating units. The best concrete realization of socialism today is the welfare state, however imperfect it is so far. Because of the human investment required the development of welfare states in the developing countries must necessarily be coupled with integrating the countries into a global analogue of the welfare state – a redistributive international economic order.

Aside from these considerations, however, and independently of the appropriateness of particular economic policies in helping the Third World move toward people-oriented development, the abolition of arms trade (or arms transfer masquerading as "aid") is an absolute imperative, just as emancipation from crippling drug addiction is an indispensable prerequisite for physical and mental health of a human being.

VII. CANADA'S POSITION IN A NEW WORLD ORDER

We suggested at the outset that the end of the confrontation between the superpowers may presage a new phase of history marked by eventual elimination of war as a global institution. Since this hope was expressed the world went to war. We got a glimpse of a world order that is both new and old. What is new is that the U.S. interventions in the Third World can no longer be justified in Cold War terms. Nicaragua is still only 48 hours drive from Texas. But the argument that Nicaragua is a potential staging area for the invasion of the U.S. by the Soviet Union won't wash any more. Leaders in the Third World who have displeased the United States can no longer be called tools of the Kremlin. A different label must now be affixed to them: Saddam, Gadhafi, Noriega, or Ortega, or whoever dares to make faces at Uncle Sam is now portrayed as a latter day Hitler or a madman in his own right.

On the other hand, the order is envisaged as the same old order. Its rationale was stated with disarming frankness by George Kennan, the architect of the containment policy, back in 1948 when he was on the State Department Policy Planning Staff. He wrote:

We have about 50% of the world's wealth, but only 6.3% of its population . . . In this situation we cannot fail to be the object of envy and resentment. Our real task . . . is to devise a pattern of relationships which permit us to maintain this disparity without positive detriment to our national security.

To do so we will have to dispense with all sentimentality . . . We need not deceive ourselves . . . We can afford the luxury of altruism and world benefaction . . . We should cease to talk about values and vague . . . unreal objectives such as human rights, raising standards of living and democratization. The day is not far off when we are going to have to deal in straight power concepts. The less we are hampered by idealistic slogans, the better.[53]

However, Kennan's advice was not taken. To be sure, actions based on straight power concepts have been evident throughout the Cold War. And almost immediately after the demise of the Cold War, they broke out with unprecedented ferocity. However, Kennan's suggestion about dropping idealistic slogans was not followed. President Bush explained starting a major war by invoking images of a struggle between good and evil and calling for God's blessing. Why? Possibly because frank talk about preserving the disparity between the U.S. and the world's poor and brandishing the wherewithal to enforce it, which may have been impressive in 1948, is no longer politically healthy. Its most probable effect would be to accelerate the already evident tide in support of Iraq by the world's poor. This support may, of course, dissipate with Iraq's defeat, but it will almost certainly be inherited by the next Third World leader who challenges the United States.

By the time this is published, the world scene may again be quite different. We believe, however, that certain trends that have become manifest in recent history are irreversible. This statement is based on an analysis and interpretation of these trends with special emphasis on their implication for Canada. We assume that the present severe setback to the cause of global peace notwithstanding, the trend toward a New World Order (as it was envisaged before the outbreak of the Gulf War) will be resumed. Our first task, then is to bring this historical trend into focus.

The Nation State and the "Realist" School of Political Science

A powerful impetus to political integration has been traditionally the perception of a common enemy. It is this perception that was usually largely responsible for the awareness of communalities, appreciation of common history, and identification with those who shared it. Indeed, the nation state is to this day widely regarded as the most stable political unit within which elimination of violent conflict can be achieved. The so-called "realist" school of political science rests squarely on this assumption. Consequently the "world order" is perceived as a conglomerate of sovereign states, each pursuing its "national interest." Further, it is assumed within the framework of the "realist" school that the overarching interest of each sovereign state is to preserve or extend its power vis-a-vis other states.

Henry Morgenthau, a prominent exponent of the "realist" school of political science suggested that power, its accumulation, distribution, use, etc. ought to be a central concept of political science in the same way as wealth, its production, distribution, consumption, etc. is a central concept of economics. "Rationality" in the context of national policy is identified by Morgenthau as the prudent use of power in the pursuit of "national interest", which is itself defined in terms of power.

The "realist" view does not exclude the cooperation between nation states, but conceives of such cooperation as an ad hoc arrangement, for example, in the context of a military alliance, which is formed or dissolved according to perceptions of a common enemy. Typically such enemies are states or blocs of states.

The so-called "Concert of Europe", an alliance of England, France, Austria, Prussia, and Russia, formed in 1815, was an exception. After Napoleon's defeat, the "enemy" was perceived by the Great Powers of that time as "revolution." The fact that the "concert" was defunct five years later speaks for the overwhelming dominance of the sovereign state as the embodiment of power and of power as the embodiment of national interest. "Common security" in those days was interpreted as the security of power elites from revolutionary upheavals. As it became clear that the interest of one power was by no means threatened by insurrections against another (sometimes on the contrary), the Concert fell apart.[54]

Only after World War I was an attempt made at integrating nation states into a collective security system where the perceived "common enemy" was neither a particular state or alliance (as from the perspective of conventional military blocs) nor aspirations of a people to autonomy (as from the perspective of the Holy Alliance spawned by the Concert of Europe) but any state initiating aggression. In fact, the idea could be said to have been born that war itself should be designated as the common enemy. The provisions of the Charter of the League of Nations give expression to this idea, where they invoke the obligation of sovereign states to resort to peaceful resolution of conflicts.

The League of Nations lasted twenty years, four times longer than the Concert of Europe. It began to fall apart in the 1930s when it proved to be powerless to stop Japan's aggression in Asia, Italy's in Africa, then Germany's in Europe.

The inadequacy of the League of Nations as a catalyst of global integration was not confined to the lack of enforcement machinery against aggression, nor the lack of political will. Broader than the Concert of Europe, it was still entirely eurocentric. It was still taken for granted by the "Powers" that European politics was world politics, that if a lasting peace was established in Europe, "order" could be kept throughout the world with the European powers "in loco parentis" with regard to the people eventually to become "civilized".

The United Nations has the potential of avoiding the principal sources of ineffectiveness of its predecessors. It has an in-principle adequate enforcement machinery to insure collective security. Furthermore, the United Nations is truly universal. With the break-up of the colonial system (in the political sense), no political unit that can reasonably claim to be a state is excluded. Whether the United Nations commands enough political will to fulfill its promise as a catalyst of global integration remains to be seen.

Canada's Role in the United Nations

An important factor in Canada's commitment to the goals of the U.N. has been the quality of our appointments to the body. The Mulroney government's appointment of Stephen Lewis as ambassador was an example of the non-partisan commitment to the U.N. which gave us a consistent and continuously strong voice there.

As in many other areas of policy, however, the greatest weakness of our record at the United Nations is our continued support of the United States' militarism. Our consistent failure to support nuclear freeze resolutions is an example of missed opportunities to distinguish between being a friend and ally of the United States and a geopolitical satellite. Douglas Roche, former Canadian Ambassador for Disarmament at the U.N. writes of the pressure which the U.S. brought to bear on him to avoid criticizing American policy.

At one of my first meetings in 1984, I ended by noting the need for better resolutions to end the arms race. At the conclusion, the U.S. ambassador privately remonstrated with me 'that the U.S. is not engaged in an arms race.' He reported this exchange to officials in Washington, who immediately lodged a complaint against me with the Canadian government.[55]

Roche does not comment on the coincidence of the year in which this incident occurred with the title of Orwell's famous novel (*Nineteen Eight-Four*). But the U.S. ambassador might as well have quoted from it directly: "War is Peace."

It is vital for our representatives to express an alternative to the American view of the world and to remonstrate in turn with their U.S. counterparts over such intimidating tactics.

Ever since its inception, the effectiveness of the United Nations as a peace-keeping institution has been crippled by the veto power conferred upon each of the "Great Powers" (regarded "great" because of their supposed exclusive possession of the power of total destruction). The idea of the veto appeared "realistic" in view of the fact that no "Great Power" was expected to be coerced into taking action against its perceived interest.

In the first 28 years of the United Nations, the Soviet Union vetoed 104 Security Council resolutions, while the United States vetoed none. In the next 16 years, however, a very different picture emerged. The Soviet Union vetoed only 10 Security Council Resolutions, while the United States vetoed 42. All in all, superpower vetoes were by far the most frequent obstacles to collective security actions by the United Nations: 156 vetoes in 44 years. By way of comparison, the United Kingdom used the veto 14 times during that period, France 19 times, and China 4 times (all by the representative of Taiwan).[56]

Although in using the veto power, the "Big Five" impaired the effectiveness of the United Nations as a peace keeping body, they were within their rights as specified in the U.N. Charter Defying the rulings of the International Court of Justice, on the other hand, was a flagrant obstruction of a process by which collective security could be institutionalized. The Court is the principal judiciary body of the United Nations. Resort to it in case of conflict between nations amounts to replacing the tyranny of the strong and violent by the rule of law. Hence by-passing it or defying its decisions amounts to obstructing efforts to introduce civility into the incipient global society. The argument that world law is ineffectual amounts to a self-realizing assumption. If it is perceived as such, it thereby becomes a dead letter and justifies the cynical dismissal of treaties as agreements to be kept only as long as they serve one's national interests.

In 1984 Nicaragua instituted proceedings against the United States relating to the responsibility of the latter for military and paramilitary actions against it. These actions included explicit acts of war, such as mining Nicaraguan harbours. In considering a case before it, the International Court of Justice first addresses the question of whether it possesses the requisite jurisdiction. If it decides that it has, it proceeds to examine the merits of the case and to pass judgement. The jurisdiction of the Court in the proceedings instituted by Nicaragua were challenged by the United States. The Court affirmed its jurisdiction, whereupon the United States refused to participate in the proceedings, and the case was tried on its merits without it.

The findings included a rejection of the argument of "self-defence" put forward by the United States and a statement to the effect that the United States has violated the obligations imposed by customary international law, as well as obligations imposed by other treaties. It then proceeded to impose a reparation to be rendered by the U.S. to Nicaragua. The dates of submitting a Memorial were fixed. Nicaragua submitted its Memorial on March 29, 1988, the prescribed time limit. The United States ignored its time limit.

The failures of international bodies are much more publicised than the successes. The peace-keeping scores of collective security blocs are by no means vacuous. Some successes were scored where the interests of major powers were not threatened or where the prospect of having to apply collective sanctions did not loom. Thus, the League of Nations settled the Swedish-Finnish dispute over Aland Islands, held plebiscites to determine the status of Upper Silesia, supervised population exchanges between Greece, Turkey and Bulgaria, etc. The United Nations was able to bring about several cease-fires, notably in the Middle East, in Kashmir, and, after two years of negotiations, in Korea.

Between 1946 and July 1, 1988 the International Court of Justice was called upon to deal with 53 cases. Of these twenty-two have been directly settled by the Court's adjudication. In others, the Court declared the question moot. This decision, too, helped the conflicting parties to arrive at a settlement. In six cases, the Court decided that it had no jurisdiction. This decision, too, had a positive effect in providing a cooling off period. In a number of these cases settlement was arrived at "out of court". In sum, the performance of the International Court of Justice as a conflict resolving body is impressive.

Of even greater significance is the potential impact of Court decisions on public attitudes toward the rule of law on the global scale. The case Nicaragua vs. United States is particularly important in this respect. A number of influential American lawyers, among them the President of the American Society for International Law censured the behaviour of the United States. Several articles on the case appeared in the prestigious *American Journal of International Law*. Judge Nagerendra Singh of the International Court of Justice quotes the following:

. . . the United States would do well to weigh the issue's implications for achieving the goal of an ordered international society in which international law and international adjudication, not force, are ascendant.[57]

Judge Singh goes on:

A number of private individuals in the United States, misled by inaccurate press reports that the Court had already awarded Nicaragua compensation, sent cheques to the Registrar by way of contribution thereto. All the cheques were, of course, politely returned to the senders, since the Court had not yet awarded reparation, and in any case individuals were not required to pay. This incident is mentioned as highly indicative of the respect for the judicial process and the rule of law among the public of the United States of America. This is indeed a feature of the legal transition which is a basis of Anglo-Saxon civilization and a very encouraging one indeed being most worthy of attention. There is respect for the Court in the minds of individuals and, by and large, public opinion can be said to give it support. However, the same cannot be said of all the Governments of the International Community.[58]

The middle powers, Canada among them, are in a favourable position to use all the influence they can muster to enhance the authority and prestige of the United Nations, in particular of the International Court of Justice. Not being "great powers," the middle powers will ordinarily not be tempted to throw their weight around and to rationalize strong arm tactics by appeal to the prerogatives of the mighty. On the other hand, not being small and weak, they can hardly be accused of appealing to the rule of law simply as a matter of protecting themselves against the strong and ruthless.

Until fall, 1990, Canada was a middle power enjoying a fairly justified reputation as a peace keeper and hence was in an especially favourable position to act as a proponent of the rule of law on the global scale. Unfortunately, Canada's reputation as peace keeper was seriously impaired when Canada immediately followed the lead of the United States in threatening the resolution of the Gulf crisis by war. The war in the Gulf broke out largely as a result of provocative actions by the United States in the form of mounting threats essentially cutting off ways by which Saddam Hussein might have been able to retreat and save face.

The consensus of the five permanent members of the Security Council in imposing mandatory sanctions on Iraq for aggression against Kuwait might have initiated a new era. It might have established the effectiveness of the Security Council in forcing conflict resolution without recourse to war. Instead, aside from the enormous cost in human lives and resources, the unleashing of a devastating attack on Iraq has served to re-affirm the legitimacy of war in an age when it presents a mortal danger to humanity.

The Security Council's role in a new era will be enhanced if it takes responsibility for anticipating threats to international peace and security rather than only reacting to them. This could be done through annual summit level meetings of the members at which they would identify potential crises and discuss measures to prevent them. Canada should work towards instituting such meetings.

If the name had not been pre-empted, the United Nations could more accurately be called the United States, as it is political entities, not cultural ones, that are primarily represented in it. It has been estimated that the world has about eight thousand identifiably separate cultures. But it has only 159 independent states.[60] The issues of national identification as recognized by the United Nations in terms of peoples' "self-determination" and "cultural rights," and complaints about states' behaviour in this regard are investigated for constructive discussion of the problems faced by member states because of cultural and ethnic diversity in their populations. Virtually all states experience these problems, and some greater understanding may be attainable by sharing experiences. Canada would have a great deal to offer and to learn from such discussions.

Canada should work to expand and empower women's organizations at the United Nations and to increase their weight among our representatives. Clear recognition should be continually given to the role of women in the search for peace, social justice, and development. In particular, the value of feminist perspectives in building a more humane world order should be emphasized.

At the same time, it should be recognized that there are serious barriers to equality and security for women in Canadian society. Addressing these problems openly and actively at home will give Canada the authority to provide leadership on women's rights at the United Nations.

The coming decade may be a time when the United Nations can become a widely recognized and effective institution for the solution of global problems. Canada, as one of its earliest and most significant supporters, can provide leadership in this crucial period.

NATO

The first three statements of the preamble to the North Atlantic Treaty Organization asserts commitments to the goals of the United Nations, to the preservation of democracy, individual liberty, the rule of law, and stability in the North Atlantic area. The first clause of the fourth statement reveals the substantive goal of the alliance: "The allies are resolved in their effort for collective defence." Except for this purpose (i.e., readiness to undertake collective military action), there is nothing in the goals mentioned in the preamble that is not served by other institutions. That is to say, if the need for collective defence of the North Atlantic area no longer exists, neither does the need for the alliance. Specifically, if, as NATO spokesmen now affirm, the Soviet Union is no longer a threat to the nations comprising NATO, the question arises: What nation is a threat? With the formal dissolution of the Warsaw Pact, NATO has lost its raison d'être. Those who maintain that the alliance should continue to exist have the obligation of specifying reasonable grounds for preserving it. In the absence of such, the continued existence of the military alliance can be attributed only to ideational inertia discussed above (cf. Chapter II). Therefore, if the dissolution of NATO is delayed, Canada should simply leave it.

Relations with Europe

The events that took place in Europe in 1989 portend an awakening of a new consciousness, a realization of Europe's mission in heralding the ultimate unification of humanity.

The heritage of Europe includes both good and evil. When we speak of European culture, we must include both Erasmus and Machiavelli, both Einstein and Hitler. When we speak of Christianity, we must include both martyrs and inquisitors, both Francis of Assissi and Roderigo Borgia, the master of intrigue and murderer, who became Pope Alexander VI. When we speak of Communism, we must include people as far apart ideologically as Marx, Stalin, and Gorbachev, and when we speak of science, we must be aware of all of its gifts, the gifts of life and the gifts of death.

If the present upheaval in Europe represents a regeneration, what is being regenerated?

We can discern two aspects of European culture, which, most will agree, can be justifiably called her unique contribution, namely, science and democracy. By science we mean modern science, which enters upon the stage of history in 16th century

Europe. It is distinguished from folk science, that is, practices learned by experience to bring about specific desirable results. It differs also from antique science, which did not include the experimental method. Modern science was created in consequence of a merger between rigorous deduction (invented by ancient Greeks) and handling material things, something that until the Renaissance was regarded proper only for slaves, artisans, and, perhaps, artists. Today we call this merger the integration of theory and practice.

The other unique European contribution was democracy. Again, certain features of democracy have existed among primitive cultures. Also some religions, in propagating the idea of human brotherhood and equality nurtured the needs of the democratic ideal. However it was in Europe that the idea of democracy took on concrete forms as a way of organizing cooperation in large complex societies without coercion.

Both ideational products of European civilization – science and democracy – rest on a common principle, namely "unity in diversity," an apparent amalgam of opposites, as dialecticians are fond of interpreting progress-generating processes. In modern science such a process underlies generalizations of theories. Evidence apparently contradicting an established theory is brought into harmony with it by formulating a more general theory which embodies the older one as a special case. Democracy is characterized by peaceful co-existence of a wide range of beliefs, tastes, convictions, and commitments. Indeed religious tolerance was one of the early achievements of incipient democracies.

Explicit commitment to unity in diversity underlies the post-Cold War idea of a united Europe, a new type of political entity, transcending the apparently unbreachable limit of integration – the nation state. The recently created Conference for Security and Cooperation in Europe (CSCE) is committed to this process.

The integration of Europe transcends both the system of alliances and the so-called "collective security" system. Alliances were supposed to produce stability of the international system by a "balance of power" and the frequently associated idea of keeping peace by "deterrence." Historical experience has shown that this way of "keeping peace" is bound to fail. A collective security system avoids the traditional practice manifested in alliances of designating states as "friendly" or "hostile." Theoretically a collective security system is a universal alliance (cf. Concert of Europe and the League of Nations). However, a collective security system does sanction collective action against an aggressor, including war. The collective security supposed to have been provided by the old League of Nations was never realized, and this failure eventually killed the League. Collective security, arrangements of the United Nations, did lead to concrete measures in a number of instances, including two horrendously destructive wars (in Korea and in the Gulf), which puts "collective security" as a peace-keeping method in question.

The CSCE is apparently committed to *common* security, which differs essentially from collective security in the sense that it depends not on the threat to "punish the aggressor" but on creating conditions in which no one is tempted to become an aggressor. Common security entails trust building and creating a pervasive infrastructure of international cooperation.

If CSCE succeeds in making NATO as obsolete as the now defunct Warsaw Pact, we may hope that a region of peace will have attained a critical size to enable it to expand and incorporate the entire planet.

At a recent conference on European Nuclear Disarmament, some misgivings were voiced about this prospect of a united Europe, particularly by delegates from the Third World. Specifically, they anticipated reduction of aid to developing countries in consequence of diverting resources to Eastern Europe and the Soviet Union. More profound misgivings concerned the prospect of cultural imperialism, attending the growing economic dominance of Europe.

Third World countries are represented in world conferences primarily by intellectuals, understandably concerned not only with physical suffering of their people but also with their aspirations to dignity and to cultural identity, aspirations impaired or altogether destroyed by colonialism and neo-colonialism. These delegates did not share the optimistic, self-congratulatory mood of the West manifested in the short interval between the end of the Cold War and the Gulf crisis.

The accusation of "eurocentrism" is sometimes leveled at those who see a unified Europe embarking on a "mission" of spreading peace and prosperity over the planet. The charge is not without foundation and must be squarely faced. People of good will in the West must realize that aspirations to cultural autonomy are just as vital as the need for personal autonomy. And surely they must divest themselves of all traces of patronizing attitudes towards the dispossessed. On the other hand, people of good will in the Third World should realize that celebration of particular contributions of Europe to world culture does not of itself amount to eurocentrism. This is especially true of the particular contributions mentioned above. The positive features of science and democracy can be incorporated into any culture as long as well being and dignity of human beings remain aspirations in that culture. When we speak of making science and democracy everyone's heritage, we speak of the emancipating potential of these products of civilization.

The emancipating features of science and democracy have been obscured by degrading and destructive by-products. In the case of science, these are obvious – death technologies and power addiction leading to the degradation of the planet. Democracy, too, is perverted by identifying it with its outward forms rather than with its fundamentals – meaningful participation of people in arriving at decisions and policies that affect their lives. The emancipating potential of science is not confined to eliminating the need for debilitating and degrading drudgery and with it the temptation of exploiting other people's labour. Science is a source of enlightenment, that is, freedom from delusions not only in interpreting the physical universe but also in inculcating self-knowledge and the nature of human societies in the light of historical experience and penetrating analysis. This enlightenment, as well as democracy, also contributes to the ideal of unity in diversity. Canada's commitment to this ideal (multiculturalism) should be an inducement for joining the European common security system.

Organization of American States

Some ten Latin American countries have divested themselves of dictatorships during the last decade. Moreover, the composition of the OAS has changed. Nearly all the Commonwealth countries of the Caribbean have joined. Reinstatement of Cuba has become a possibility.[59]

Supporters of Canadian membership in the OAS maintain that it will improve the climate of increased trade. Minister of External Affairs Joe Clark has pointed out that the volume of bilateral trade with Latin America already exceeds that with Southeast Asia and China combined and that the potential increase is even greater. Not the least important factor in this prospect is the rapid growth of population in Latin America. Projections indicate that, by the end of the century, the population of Central and South America will be double that of the European Community.

More than in any other area, Canada's contribution to a just world order depends on the role it plays in the Organization of American States (OAS). It is in respect to Latin America that Canada has on occasion shown some readiness to withdraw support from the heavy-handed policy of the United States. We have continued to maintain diplomatic and trade relations with Cuba. On occasions criticism was voiced of the proxy war waged by the United States against Nicaragua. Activities of the death squads in El Salvador, the terrorist branch of the government supported by the United States, were unequivocally condemned. As a member of OAS Canada can make these exceptions to U.S. domination of Latin America count.

One of the cornerstones of the OAS is Article 15, which reads:

No State or group of States has the right to intervene directly or indirectly, for any reason whatsoever, in the internal or external affairs of any other States. The foregoing principle prohibits not only armed force but also any other form of interference or attempted threat against the personality of the State or against its political, economic, and cultural elements.

It was the crass violations of this article that were largely responsible for the tarnished image of the OAS. If the changes during the past decade are given additional momentum, the organization could be eventually fitted into a just world order.

An important step forward could be the removal of features that tend to make the organization a military alliance. For example, the Rio Treaty would require every signatory to treat an attack on one member state as an attack on all – a collective security arrangement. The trouble with such an arrangement is the opportunity it gives for interpreting certain kinds of political developments as "attacks" or, at any rate as "preparations for attack." This has been essentially the interpretation placed by the U.S. on political changes in Cuba and in Nicaragua. This interpretation was used to justify interventions as "self defence." The Rio Treaty lapsed when Jamaica did not sign and died during the Falklands War. (Had the Treaty been in force, all American states would have been obliged to defend Argentina against Britain.)

A step toward incorporating Latin America in a just world order would be to make common security (instead of militarily oriented collective security) a foundation of the Organization of American States. The Conference on Security and Cooperation in Europe might provide a model for this foundation.

Canada can play a constructive role in this process if it turns its attention to the plight of the hemisphere and its causes. The demise of some of the explicit and brutal dictatorships should not detract our attention from the steady worsening of the economic conditions in the poor Americas. The decline during the last decade was catastrophic. For example, the UN Economic Commission on Latin America and the Caribbean reports that the proportion of the Guatemalan population living in extreme poverty increased from 45% in 1985 to 76% in 1988. In rural areas, 13% of children under five die of illnesses related to malnutrition. The precipitous impoverishment has swept throughout Central America. According to a report of the Interamerican Development Bank, the per capita income in that region has fallen at the end of the 1980s to the level of 1971 in Guatemala, 1961 in El Salvador, 1973 in Honduras, 1965 in Nicaragua, 1974 in Costa Rica, 1982 in Panama.[61]

It was during the 1980s that the interventionist policies of the United States became especially oppressive. They were clearly a reaction to the populist movements that led to the initial democratization of some Latin American regimes, and their result has been to paralyze social and economic reforms that might have been developed in the wake of the political changes.

Canadian membership in the OAS could be a factor in integrating Latin America into a just world order, if Canada's policies provided a counterweight to U.S. domination.

Globalism and Globalization

"Globalism" should be an appropriate designation for an ideology which assigns the highest priority to dealing with paramount global issues – peace, environmental protection, and a just world order based on people-oriented sustainable development in poor countries. A similar sounding term, "globalization" refers to something else – any process that transcends national boundaries. Not all such processes are conducive to actions directed toward coping with the paramount global problems. For instance, we have pointed out that the war system has become globalized in the sense that its national components have become so strongly interdependent that they can be viewed as integrated into a global war machine. Also the world arms trade represents the globalization of w a r establishments. In our view, this globalization process has produced a lethal threat to humanity. Other globalization processes have both positive and negative features. Among these is economic globalization.

Awareness of the new technologies of communication, production, and transportation along with political stability in much of the industrialized world have made multinational enterprises profitable in many economic sectors. As is the case with all historical change, this development presents both opportunities and dangers, and gives rise to some opposition of interests among various groups of people affected by it.

In order to understand the political issues that arise from economic globalization, it will be useful to recall briefly the history of the relationship between national corporations and their societies. The benefits of dramatically expanded production made possible by the Industrial Revolution were limited at first by severe and sudden damage to the independence of working people and to the environment and by the application of new technologies to military production.

Through political actions, the world's democracies have to some extent attenuated the destructive effects of industrialism. Unionism, labour and environmental laws, and international peace agreements have helped to produce societies in which people are willing to work and do not actively oppose the status quo. The interests of most people in these societies have been sufficiently protected to make them think of corporations as socially valuable institutions.

In other countries, by contrast, people who control resources and production have been protected from the those outside their circles by various forms of coercion and oppression. Organizations which have attempted to represent the powerless have consistently faced political exclusion, often violence, throughout most of the world.

With the globalization of capital, the potential for a national government to protect the interests of its people has been severely limited. As pointed out above, multinational corporations are not dependent on favourable business conditions in any one country, particularly a small country, since they can simply withdraw in response to any unacceptable efforts to regulate them. In recent decades, democratic regimes have emerged in many countries; but elected governments have been by and large powerless to use their resources for the benefit of their entire populations. If national democracy continues to be unable to limit the destructive activities of international capital, we will have to place our hopes on international democracy. In addition to efforts in the United Nations to establish and enforce global rights and standards of common security, an attempt should be made to put human issues on the agenda of the General Agreement on Tariffs and Trade (GATT).

This body is an important institution which recognizes that states have responsibilities to each other to cooperate in building and maintaining a healthy world economy. We would like to see the organization's mandate expanded to include social issues that are relevant to world trade.

For instance, interference with the organization and effective operation of labour unions is an unfair trade practice. The resulting low labour costs for export goods generate an unfair price advantage over goods produced by union labour in other countries. Lack of environmental and safety regulations is similarly a political problem which should be addressed as an unfair trade practice, by raising these issues at GATT. Canada can help set an agenda for social change in an organization with which it has strong incentive to cooperate because of the economic importance of good trade relations.

While multilateral agreements would be a valuable step to improving international cooperation on vital human issues, we should also advocate a system of global law to which international corporations could be held accountable. It will be essential once international standards are agreed upon that the enforcement of the standards not be left solely in the hands of the national governments.

In sum, Canada's position in a new world order can be a position of leadership if Canada adopts policies conducive to the advancement of globalism in its humanity-oriented sense.

VIII.   IMPLICATIONS FOR DOMESTIC POLICY

Defence and Security

A nation's values are reflected in large measure in the way the people spend their money. And since a great deal of their money is spent by their governments, the way it is spent reflects the values of governments. If the government is democratic, its values and those of most of the people should coincide at least to a certain extent. This places a responsibility on the government to order its priorities in relation to the priorities of its citizens.

The priorities revealed in the allocation of the people's money should be defended by cogent arguments. In particular, policies related to defence should be justified by serious considerations. Such justification was offered recently by General John de Chestelain, who said:

> . . . we have not today, nor can we hope to have in the foreseeable future, the population and the resource base necessary to defend unaided our national territory . . .[62]

Although this premise is widely accepted and promoted by those whose interests depend on military alliances, it is false. That Canada cannot defend itself without help is a myth. What does it mean to defend Canadian territory? Whoever suggests "defending Canadian territory" must suggest concrete threats to it. What sort of threats are they? From whom? If from the Soviet Union, as has been assumed during the past four decades, this must mean that the Soviet government (N.B., the present Soviet government or one likely to replace it) is planning . . . to do what? Invade Canada's territory? Since it is the military experts who are most insistent on pointing out the "threat" to Canada, they have the obligation to describe the events threatening, for example, an invasion of Canadian territory. Does that mean that they are asking people to imagine ships off the coast of Labrador or Nova Scotia with landing craft carrying troops and landing on beaches? Or, perhaps, swarms of parachutists landing on Canadian soil? Assuming the landings successful, what would the invaders undertake next? How is the glib phrase "take over the country" to be realized? The absurdity of the scenario should give pause before the oft repeated but contentless imperative "to defend Canadian territory" is accepted as a justification of the funds directed to this purpose.

Ever since all wars became "defensive" and, accordingly, all Departments of War became "Departments of Defence," all "defence needs" are sold to the public as imperatives of "security." From the vantage point of the global outlook, the only definition of "security" that does not involve a contradiction in terms is common security. Common security means the security of all nations. No nation can guarantee its own security by undermining the security of another. There is either security for all nations or there is security for none. Put another way, we are all in the same boat. It does not improve our own security if we drill a hole in the boat under a nation or a group of nations whom we regard as our adversaries. Common security rejects the pursuit of military superiority in favour of defence forces that defend rather than threaten and provoke. It means replacing nuclear terrorism with mutual defence; and it means focusing on demilitarizing international relations and on the peaceful resolution of conflicts.

The churches (the Canadian Council of Churches) in their foreign policy submission in 1985 advanced a principle of common security as a guide to an appropriate Canadian foreign and defence policy. In 1987 the Canadian Federation of University Women adopted a policy of support for the principle of common security as a basis for peace; and in early 1989, the federal government's Consultative Group recommended that Canada's approach to security be revised at both the conceptual and policy levels, and that the concept of common security be explored as a basis for this revised policy. Common security is implicit in the Brundtland Commission Report's emphasis that "security is indivisible."

The first task in designing a rational security policy for Canada is to divest ourselves of concepts that have lost all claim to validity. Because of the dependent nature of our military industrial arrangements, Canada supports the status quo. That is, we go along with the course chosen by both our U.S. dominated alliances (NATO, NORAD), which pile weapons upon weapons under the notion that this will prevent war. The intermediate Nuclear Force (INF) Treaty, signed in December 1987, removes about 2000 nuclear weapons from Europe. But the U.S. and the U.S.S.R. are still modernizing their nuclear arsenals and adding to them (at this writing) about 10 nuclear weapons daily. The INF Treaty does little in itself to promote international security. Its significance lies in the potential of further arms control agreements.

Unfortunately, the INF Treaty appears to have made little difference to our government's thinking. Now, Canadians are told, we must prepare for a long conventional war by developing a defence industrial base to build the capacity for wartime production to replace the losses and keep the conventional war running.[63]

If Canada is serious about making a contribution to international security, we must exercise our capacity for political choice, a capacity that has been much undermined by the dependent nature of Canada's military-industrial arrangements. The Defence Production Sharing Arrangements with the United States must be phased out as current contracts expire. This would allow a new 'made-in-Canada' defence policy based on the principle of common security. Such a policy would be directed not towards fighting wars (as is our current defence policy), but towards strengthening the just international order on which Canada's existence as a nation depends.[64] The military production to support a revised Canadian defence policy should then focus on the special peacetime requirements related to Canadian territory and to international peacekeeping.

Within our borders, Canada can promote a more stable world order by ensuring that Canadian territory, resources and skills, will never be used to threaten any nation. In order to do this, we must take control of our own territory. This means that Canada must have the demonstrable capacity to carry out the necessary air and sea surveillance and patrol of our territory. This would require a broad range of equipment, especially surveillance and communication equipment, which should be the focus of Canadian military production.[65]

Beyond our borders, Canada can contribute to the peaceful settlement of disputes by participating in United Nations peacekeeping missions. Canada has participated in every United Nations peacekeeping mission thus far: more than 80,000 Canadians have been involved. However, the resources available for Canadian peacekeeping forces are severely limited. It appears that External Affairs officials are apprehensive about future peacekeeping requests because of the concern that they would lead to shortages in other areas of the Armed Forces.[66] Thus, major new resources must be allocated for a standing Canadian peacekeeping force that could be integrated into a standing UN peacekeeping force as soon as such a standing UN force is established. Since peacekeeping operations depend in particular on communications, surveillance, and transport equipment, this should be the focus of Canadian military spending and production.

This approach to military production in Canada could be no less expensive to Canada than the present arrangements. However, this could be ameliorated by entering into joint production with another nation whose defence needs are similar to Canada's, e.g., a nation with a long coastline. Nevertheless, it would have to be clearly stipulated that any arms transfers would be "directed," i.e., deliberate government acts in support of articulated defence and foreign policy objectives. They would not be treated as commercial ventures.

In sum, Canadian defence policy should be based on the emerging principle of common security, which offers hope of freeing humanity from the curse of war.

Economic Policy: The Problem of Conversion

A first priority in designing an economic policy for the new phase of history is the preparation and implementation of a conversion plan. Conversion is redirection of material and human resources previously wasted in activities dictated by obsolete conceptions of security into productive channels to serve human needs.

In 1982 the United Nations General Assembly urged the member states to undertake national conversion studies to (1) describe and analyze the resources devoted to the military sector and the economic and social consequences of this resource allocation, and (2) decide on plans and preparations for conversion, i.e., the transfer of human and military resources from the military to the civil sector with a simultaneous increase in development cooperation with the Third World. Sweden was the first nation to undertake a national conversion study, and the Soviet Union announced in December 1988 that it would undertake one also.[67]

The objective of conversion is not the elimination of all military production from Canada. Its aim is "to dismantle an institutional military procurement, which (a) influences and distorts assessments of military needs and actually drives military procurement, and (b) depends for its survival on regularly repeated military contracts, and (c) relies on foreign sales that undermine constructive national policies related to peace and justice."[68]

Conversion plans and preparations in the Canadian context would mean examining the costs and consequences of our growing institutionalized military industry, developing new alternative products to replace products that have only or primarily military applications and developing markets for these alternative products. It would also mean finding new non-military markets for products that have civilian as well as military applications (for example, Pratt and Whitney engines that can be used in either military or civilian aircraft without alteration). Conversion would, in some instances, mean retraining of workers and retooling of industries, actions which would require assistance from the government.

The most important feature of Canada's military production is that it is export oriented and highly commercialized. More than 300 Canadian companies are now regular participants in the arms-export business and many more are occasional participants. The federal government, through the Defence Programs Bureau of the Department of External Affairs, promotes military exports by mounting military trade missions to countries such as South Korea, Indonesia, Thailand, and Brazil, by hosting an annual "high tech conference" in Ottawa, which brings together Canadian trade and industry representatives to develop new sales categories; and by publishing a series of glossy publications announcing the range of goods Canada has to offer or by providing Canadian exporters with up-to-date information about military sales opportunities around the world.[69]

In addition, the Canadian Commercial Corporation, a Crown corporation funded by the government, assists Canadian arms dealers through the whole process of selling abroad. As a result of Canada's commercially oriented policy, Canadian-made arms products end up in some very undesirable places: Chile, Columbia, El Salvador, Ethiopia, and Turkey. All of these are known to be human rights violators. In May 1989, the fourth of a series of international arms bazaars (ARMX), was held in Ottawa, promoted by our Departments of External Affairs and National Defence. Delegations from more than 50 countries were involved, including some with records of human rights violations. Significantly 2000 people took to the streets of Ottawa to demonstrate their protest; more than 100 were arrested for direct non-violent protest, and Ottawa City Council voted not to allow ARMX to be held again in that city. Clearly, Canadians do not want their country to become an international arms merchant. Yet this is the direction in which Canada's export-oriented military production arrangements are taking us.

Under current arrangements, the Canadian government has no control over the ultimate destination of more than half of the military commodities produced in Canada. Canadian military products are routinely sold to the U.S. (where no export permit is needed) or to other countries like Italy or Brazil for "manufacture" into larger weapons systems which are then sold to another country. Hence, Canadian military products have ended up in countries such as Iran, Iraq, and Libya. Canada should take steps to prevent this by placing its military exports to the U.S. under the export permit system and by demanding end-user permits. This would ensure that Canada's declared export control policies apply to all Canadian military products.

As for direct Canadian sales of military commodities, the Canadian government claims to have one of the most restrictive military export control policies in the world. The problem is that it is full of loopholes. Hence, Canadian military products have ended up on the battlefields in many of the wars that have taken place since 1945 and in the arsenals of human rights violators.[70]

During the years 1980-1984, 60% of Third World recipients of Canadian military commodities were cited by Amnesty International as regularly carrying out human rights violations. Even the United Nations Commission on Human Rights, under a more restricted definition of human rights violator, cited 28% of the Third World recipients of Canadian military commodities as human rights violators. Indeed the huge value of military products approved for sale during 1984-1987 (more than $1.5 billion), "combined with the upward trend to annual permit totals, suggests a loosening of Canadian export controls to human rights violators."[71]

The Canadian government – unlike the U.S. – has never revealed the details of Canadian military exports. These details are unavailable even under our so-called access to information legislation. The reasons are not related to security but to "commercial confidentiality," that is, to competitiveness of Canadian firms. No system to control the transfer of military products is likely to work effectively or have public confidence if it is carried out in secret. Thus it is essential that there be full disclosure of military and military-related exports and that these exports be subject to an annual public review and vigorous public debate.

Assuming that conversion is a prime priority of Canada's economic policy in the new phase of history, we recommend the following steps toward conversion:

1.   Undertake a national study to plan and prepare for the conversion of Canada's military industries, except those needed to supply Canada's legitimate defence needs as defined by Canada;

2.   End the promotion of military production and sales as a commercial enterprise;

3.   Regain control over Canada's military production arrangements by withdrawing from the Canada-U.S. Defence Production Sharing Arrangements (DDPSA);

4.   Eliminate the Defence Industry Production Programme and use the funds to encourage and assist Canadian military industries to convert to civilian production.

Canadian military production must be considered temporary and should be carried out on the assumption that when the particular equipment needs in question are met, the human and material resources devoted to military purpose will be redirected towards meeting human needs. Thus industrial conversion should be an integral element of all military production.

It is essential, however, that the detailed implementation of conversion be guided by an extensive Conversion Study aimed at designing ways to carry out conversion in a manner least damaging to Canadians. Such a study would be an action plan that would facilitate the smooth transition from military to civilian production.[72]

A conversion study would have numerous advantages. Specifically, it would help Canada prepare for the shrinking arms market that will inevitably accompany the end of the arms boom of the 1980s, thus avoiding major job dislocation in Canada. Moreover, it would stimulate public awareness that Canada need not be locked into permanent military spending increases and weapons sales in order to "save our economic system."[73] This would mean increased public support for conversion.

A conversion study would also pave the way for the conversion of obsolete Canadian military bases, such as the one at Summerside, PEI, to civilian use, thus avoiding major job dislocation.

Such a study would be consistent with the United Nations recommendation in 1982 that all nations should undertake a conversion study. It would also be consistent with the recommendation of the Brundtland Report for nations to turn away from the arms race and focus on human needs and the world's vast environmental problems.

A conversion study would provide substance to Canada's commitment early in 1989 to the principle of sustainable development as a priority for decisions on economic and social issues. The production of armaments or their components for economic reasons is not sustainable. Indeed, a conversion study would be a significant step toward sustainable development and would be consistent with the words of the Right Honourable Joe Clark at the United Nations Conference on the Relationship of Disarmament and Development in 1987, when he appealed for "practical cooperation" in support of "the principle which Canada assumes all participants share – namely, that less money must be spent on arms and more money must be spent on development."[74]

A conversion study would also be consistent with Canada's international image of a peacekeeper and mediator, for it would signal to the world that Canada is withdrawing its participation in the global war economy, thus setting an example to other nations to do the same.

Because military industries are capital intensive rather than labour intensive, conversion would result in more jobs for Canadians; it would also focus Canadian research and development on civilian production, thus contributing to a favourable balance of trade for Canada.

Conversion would also result in increased resources for peacekeeping forces. Indeed, conversion and peacekeeping could be the basis for a permanent Canadian peace initiative that would insure the use of Canadian territory, resources, and skills to promote common security and peace.

Tasks of Education

Before literacy became widespread, integration of the young into the human community occurred at home. As reading and writing became part of socialization, formal schooling was established and even became compulsory in many societies.

Formal education comprises three processes with different degrees of emphasis in different societies: training, indoctrination, and enlightenment. Training is supposed to confer skills, indoctrination to inculcate beliefs and attitudes, enlightenment to help develop autonomy. Skills facilitate an individual's integration in the world of work. The aim of indoctrination has been traditionally to create a population committed to the same values and loyalties. Enlightenment is supposed to confer the ability to think independently, to subject beliefs to reality testing, and to develop a sense of social responsibility by identifying self-interests with the common weal.

In educational systems controlled by an established church or a totalitarian regime, indoctrination has always been a most significant feature of education. In more or less democratic and liberal societies, indoctrination is frowned upon. Education is conceived to be conducive to independent thinking, self-realization, in short, the growth of autonomy. Ongoing criticism of an education system by "progressive" educators centres on the shortcomings of the system in that regard.

Whatever be the prevailing philosophy of education in a society, aspiration to education by a large majority of its population has been demonstrably motivated by the fact that by and large the educated have more access to higher economic and social status in a society. This is especially apparent in societies with comparatively open social mobility. In consequence, technical and professional schooling has become the most important function of the system of higher education in the industrialized world. This is especially the case in North America. Nevertheless, voices are constantly raised about the neglect of the enlightening function of education. Democracy, it is said, can function only in a society with an enlightened citizenship. Enlightenment entails awareness of physical and social realities and an ability to assess intelligently the consequences of actions. On the level of technology, competence means just that: knowledge of physical laws and their implications and the ability to understand and to predict behaviour of artifacts in the light of that knowledge. On the level of social phenomena and policies, the analogue of competence is awareness of social realities and the ability to understand the implications of social actions (including conflicts) and of policies.

In the light of what has been said here, it is clear that an enlightened citizenry in this sense has become more than a prerequisite of a functioning democracy. It is now a prerequisite of human survival since the global issues (preservation of peace, ecological responsibility, and a just world order) have assumed life and death significance.

What are the implications of the conclusion for the educational policy in Canada? Training, in any case, remains a necessary component of education, because the young need preparation for employment. Enlightenment is compatible with training, even though the two functions may compete for time, funds, etc. On the other hand, enlightenment is incompatible with indoctrination.

Some may imagine that indoctrination plays no part in modern educational systems, those not controlled by an established religion and tolerant of differing political views or social philosophies. Nevertheless, unless the crucial global issues are accorded sufficient prominence in the education system, tacit indoctrination takes place, namely the inculcation of "business as usual" attitudes in a world that can no longer afford "business as usual." If we agree that enlightenment must invoke challenges of superstitions and of conventional wisdom, failure to include such challenges in education amounts to neglect of the enlightenment function.

Of the three paramount issues discussed here (peace, environmental protection, and global justice) concern with environmental protection has made the most inroads into education. There have been two reasons for this relative success. First, of the three issues, environmental protection has struck the most sympathetic chord. It is the least controversial, at any rate with regard to its aims, which are difficult to oppose, even though controversies rage about means of implementation (which directly affect various special interests).

Second, environmental education is rather solidly rooted in the natural sciences, which because of their direct relevance to technology command considerable more respect than the social sciences or the humanities, which are more directly relevant to matters of peace and global justice.

Assuming that the development of environmental studies will go on apace and is likely to receive support, we must call attention to the present inadequacy of our educational system in creating enlightenment on matters related to global peace and global justice.

Peace Education — Objections to peace education in some circles stem in part from the assumption that it amounts to indoctrination or that the courses comprising such programmes do not satisfy the standards of academic sophistication. Neither shortcoming, whatever be its manifestations in particular cases, is inherent in the idea of peace education as it is designed for the purpose of inducing enlightenment. To begin with, a good peace education programme involves examination of conflict (including war) as well as exploration of roads to peace. The history, dynamics, issues, and consequences of conflict between human groups can be studied on a level comparable to that of any other branch of social science. In fact, examination of curricula offered in the departments of psychology, sociology, history, and political science in North American universities reveals sufficient scope to serve as a basis of a programme of peace education both broad enough and deep enough to constitute a major input toward enlightenment on matters related to war and peace, conflict, and conflict resolution. It remains to design overarching courses to show how knowledge already available can be used in the exploration of roads to peace. This goal-directed aspect of peace education need not jeopardize its standing in higher education any more than explorations of applications of natural science to, say, the development of technology or to the development of health programmes need to jeopardize the academic standing of engineering or biology faculties.

In the United States there are anywhere from 60 to 200 programmes in peace and conflict studies (depending on the criteria of scope and academic level in classifying them as such). The programmes are designed both at the undergraduate and the graduate levels. Some lead to doctoral degrees. In Canada, the number of such programmes is much smaller even relative to the size of the education sector. In contrast, over twenty extensive strategic studies programmes are presently supported by the Department of National Defence. Needless to say, although Canadian educational institutions enjoy considerable autonomy with respect to direction and content of secondary and higher education, support by government bodies is an important determinant of both direction and content. We favour active support by the government of the expansion of peace education, which now deserves full recognition as an important field with potential relevance to the development of social science in ways to enable it to deal with the paramount issues of our day.

Environmental Education — As has been said, environmental education has been successfully incorporated into the system of higher education, in some cases also in secondary education. We support its further development, especially the establishment of links between the issues of environmental protection and issues related to preservation of peace and of sustainable development. A case in point is the confrontation cited above of Turkey and Syria in which threat of violent conflict is tightly intertwined with environmental and development issues.

Education for a Just Social Order — This aspect of the enlightenment function of education may be the most difficult to realize of the three. The reasons for this have to do with curricula and with the structure and social role of educational institutions.

Issues related to a just social order are more controversial than those related to peace or environmental protection. Once the threat inherent in the very existence of genocidal weapons is understood, the proposed means of removing it can be relatively easily accepted. In the case of environmental degradation, although the proposed remedies may induce apprehension about their effects on our life style, these apprehensions may be dissipated in the process of enlightenment. But issues of social justice present special problems.

To begin with, the theoretical underpinnings of economics are more controversial than the branches of natural science dealing with environmental problems and the effects of weapons. Therefore we cannot assume that imparting scientific knowledge about the problems related to social justice can make an impact on students' thinking comparable to that made by scientific knowledge about the environment and about war. Also the measures proposed to redress injustice are more controversial from the point of view of their effectiveness than those related to peace and the environment, which have a strong objective basis in natural science.

More importantly, proposals on social justice induce greater apprehensions concerning the fate of the privileges enjoyed by the affluent than measures proposed in support of the environment and peace. Existing curricula may exacerbate this problem by ignoring social justice issues. Business administration courses which teach methods of maximizing profits without regard to social costs, for instance, or economics courses which deal strictly with macroeconomic processes without their implications for human welfare, can obfuscate social reality. Enlightenment in this area requires a great deal of work, expertise, pedagogical skill, and the personal commitment of educators to social justice.

The structural obstacles to education for social justice are related to the traditional role of educational institutions in perpetuating elite privilege. This role, at its stark extreme, is, of course, entirely inconsistent with the social justice aspect of enlightenment, as the participants in the educational process are reinforcing their own status at the expense of the rest of society.

The first and widely recognized method of solving this problem is in improving access to education through subsidies, scholarships, and measures to redress and prevent discrimination. This effort has been seriously undertaken in Canada. It has been quite successful at the elementary and secondary levels and has made notable progress in higher education as well.

In elementary and secondary schools the most serious remaining problem of access is caused by regional and local disparities in resources. School boards in poorer regions, especially in native reserves and in the Maritime provinces, must be better subsidized if the Canadian educational system is to aspire to social justice.

At the post-secondary level, the access which has been gained is in constant danger of receding as a result of budget cuts. The current level of access should be seen as a stage in the process of achieving free education. There should be a political commitment to this goal from all levels of government and a plan to achieve it eventually through permanent allocation of resources. Regressions in the form of tuition increases and higher student housing costs should be prevented by long term plans for financing.

While access to education is a necessary condition for a socially just educational system, it is not sufficient. To overcome their traditional function of service to society's elites, universities are beginning to make concrete commitments to an egalitarian society rather than merely easing admission to the elite for traditionally excluded people. A crucial component of these commitments is the creation of departments of women's and ethnic studies.

These departments have many complementary roles in the orientation of universities to social justice. They are necessary additions to curricula, as an antidote and a challenge to traditional academic worldviews. They provide positions for women and people of minority groups, so that they can develop disciplines which relate to their concerns, setting their own agendas, rather than adapting their careers to traditional academic priorities or being denied academic positions altogether.

Objections to women's and ethnic studies are sometimes raised on the grounds that there is a lack of materials on a sufficiently high academic level or that faculty appointed on the basis of gender or ethnicity may be less qualified than faculty appointed (supposedly) without regard to these facts. To some extent, these objections may be based on prejudice, but if they are sometimes reasonable, they may be easily answered. The volume and quality of material in women's and ethnic studies is rapidly growing and would be immediately further stimulated by the widespread introduction of such programmes. Similarly with regard to appointees, competence and assignment of responsibility can be expected to reinforce each other, and the opening up of academic opportunities will encourage gifted scholars to pursue careers in these fields.

Another argument in favour of female and ethnic faculty members teaching studies related to the social positions of women and ethnic minorities is analogous to the argument that a foreign language is, in general, more effectively taught by a native speaker of the language. In the case of language instruction, this is clear. Not only a technical knowledge of a language (its phonetics, grammar, etc.) but also its "feel" is an important component of competence in it, especially in such areas as poetry. The same can be said in the case of studies belonging to humanities in general. One can defend a similar position in the case of studies classified as "social" on the grounds that the technical analysis and a positivistic approach do not exhaust the effective methods in developing and teaching the social sciences. Specifically, instruction by members of social groups studied can induce enlightenment beyond that provided by standard courses taught by faculty members not belonging to these groups.

Similar considerations apply to research, where the knowledge to be disseminated through education is generated. Professor Ursula Franklin of the University of Toronto is recognized as an outstanding scientist working in metallurgy, a field unequivocally belonging to "hard" science, where only demonstrable "facts" (and not intuitive insights) are accepted as "legal tender." She has the following to say about the possible contribution of women *as women* to science.

. . . Science, by its very nature, separates knowledge from experience. This is its strength, as it moves from the specific to the general, in order to derive laws considered applicable to all appropriate situations.

However, this separation is also science's greatest weakness. Research is carried out in an unrealistically simplified environment, eliminating more often than not variables that are essential if we are to answer questions in context. Why? Because for traditionally trained scientists, researching living systems is "messy." How can you conduct an experiment without being able to isolate – or even identify – major variables?

A feminist researcher may be less easily frightened away from tackling questions too complex for "good science." Why not, she might say, take those who provide experiences seriously and make them partners, rather than neutral subjects of research.

Such an approach would entail designing and revising the research questions, the protocol, the procedures, and the modes of observation, the controls and tests in conjunction with the subjects of study. Subjective and possibly introspective observations . . . would have to be taken seriously. Thus, the subject of the research, not the researcher, would be called upon to verify how representative his or her experiences are.[75]

A significant benefit of women's and ethnic studies in universities will be the inclusion of both people and ideas reflecting the diversity of society. The development of the academic community which will result will greatly contribute to the ability of academia to be a force for social justice and will greatly enhance the relevance of education.

The enlightenment goals of education are best served by integration of different areas of study. We have discussed three areas that are especially relevant to understanding our changing world: problems of establishing a durable peace; problems of providing a livable environment to leave to our children; problems of establishing a just world order. We cited the confrontation between Turkey and Syria to show how an environmental issue can become an instigator of an international conflict. It is becoming increasingly evident that the promiscuous use of nuclear energy is a nexus between militarization and environmental threat. And of course, the vast disparity of access to the bounties of the planet interact both with degradation of human resources and with chronic violence. Finally, the explosion in the Gulf has shown how the power appetite of a Third World leader, inflamed and nurtured by the global war machine, can activate that machine with all the horrendous consequences this entails.

One of the most important tasks of education in preparation for the next millennium is that of providing a focus for integrating human concerns.

IX. SUMMARY AND RECOMMENDATIONS

The views expressed in this document address the concerns of the majority of Canadians. Already in 1987 a poll published by the Ottawa-based North-South Institute revealed the following hierarchy of concerns among the Canadian public:

1. Pollution and the environment.
2. Major world disease.
3. Poverty and hunger.
4. The possibility of nuclear war.
5. Apartheid and human rights.
6. World economic collapse.

Besides these the concerns that outranked "Soviet aggression" (to take a basis of comparison) in 1987 were (a) erratic U.S. policy; (b) world population growth; and (c) Third World debt.

We have given special emphasis to the necessity of disengaging Canadian policies from those of the United States, because we believe that although the danger of war between the superpowers has receded since 1987, the inertia of American thinking still impedes its total removal. The danger of a devastating war will persist as long as the disarmament process is impeded and as long as the United States banks on unilateral intervention in pursuit of its own perceived interests. As Thomas G. Weiss put it, "Now that the Soviets have embraced UN and other international organizations, the only superpower left to be convinced is the U.S.A."[76]

The proposed agenda for the last decade of the millennium can be summarized in the following recommendations addressed to the government or to whatever groups, organizations, or individuals are in a position to undertake relevant initiatives.

1.   Canada should regard itself as a member of a nascent human community. Its policies should be directed toward goals that are compatible with the fulfillment of fundamental human needs.

2.   Survival is a fundamental human need. The burgeoning growth of the global war machine threatens the survival of the human race. The dismantling of this machine should be a major goal of Canadian policies.

3.   The abolition of nuclear weapons and other weapons of total destruction is a global imperative. Canada should be committed to this goal.

4.   A prerequisite for the abolition of nuclear weapons is the preservation and extension of the Nuclear Non-proliferation Treaty. Canadian foreign policy should be directed toward this end.

5.   A comprehensive Nuclear Test Ban Treaty is a prerequisite of preserving and extending the Nuclear Non-proliferation Treaty. Canadian foreign policy should be directed to that end.

6.   Canada should have an independent foreign policy. In particular, Canadian foreign policy should be decoupled from those aspects of U.S. foreign policy that obstruct measures aimed at dismantling the global war machine. Further, Canadian foreign policy should be decoupled from those aspects of U.S. foreign policy that aim to dominate other countries either through direct intervention or through other pressures.

7.   Environmental protection and environmental recovery should be among the central goals of Canadian policies, foreign and domestic.

8.   In designing environmental policies, the tight interdependence of all the components of the environment should be kept in mind: the atmosphere, the hydrosphere, the geosphere, the biosphere, and the noosphere. The entire environment belongs

to the entire human race. Canadian policies should be based on the assumption that the "health" of every component of the environment depends on that of every other component and the welfare of any sector of humanity depends on the welfare of every other sector.

9. Even as the danger of war between countries of the developed world becomes remote, it should be kept in mind that the chronic violence in the Third World is likely to remain unabated in the immediate future. The roots of that violence should be clearly perceived. Among them is the continuing exploitative relationship between the affluent and the impoverished worlds. Partnership should replace both exploitation and paternalistic charity as the basis of the relationship between the developed and the developing worlds.

10. The aim of aid to the Third World should be support of sustainable development. In the pursuit of this objective, the choice of partners should be decoupled from considerations related to commercial advantage and also from those related to geopolitics. The choice of partners should, however, be consistent with support of sustainable development and its goals – the development of a just social order. Countries with regimes genuinely devoted to these goals should be the preferred partners.

11. On the stage of world politics, Canada should work for strengthening the authority and prestige of the United Nations, particularly in its peace-keeping role.

12. In the activities of international organizations, Canada should represent the stand that autonomy of nations or cooperative regions is not incompatible with limitations placed on certain aspects of national sovereignty, in particular, on the unlimited right to prepare for and engage in war and on the unlimited right to actions affecting adversely any component of the environment.

13. All of us should take a fresh look at the role of education in the present and nascent phase of history. Initiatives to direct the educational process toward goals consistent with human needs should be left to the educators. However, the government and

other public institutions can play a vital role in providing support and broadening the access to sources of enlightenment.

14. All of us should recognize the role of women in peace and development work and support their increased participation in decision-making processes.

15. All of us should work toward welding a broad coalition of Canadians determined to cope energetically and intelligently with the paramount global problems of our age.

POSTSCRIPT

On February 28, 1991, the fighting in the Middle East was suspended. Commenting on the implications of the Gulf War, Douglas Roche, Canadian Ambassador for Disarmament from 1983-1989 wrote:

> When the Bush administration turned its back on the United Nations and launched the ground war in the Gulf, a new era opened.
> Now we live at a time when the one superpower in the world scorns negotiations and uses its military might to get its way. This has enormous implications for the entire world.
> Not only did the U.S. give the back of its hand to Mikhail Gorbachev's offers to fuse the American and Soviet plans for Iraq's withdrawal from Kuwait, it rejected its own heritage. Thirty years ago, in a shining moment of U.S. history, John F. Kennedy declared in his inaugural address:
> 'Let us never negotiate out of fear, but let us never fear to negotiate.'
> Six presidents later, George Bush has made it clear that military power, not diplomacy, is the route to a new world order.

The aftermath of the Gulf War will surely vindicate our emphasis on the necessity of decoupling Canada's policies from those of the present and recent American administrations. Not only have these policies prevented the organization of global efforts to cope with the paramount global problems, but they have actually aggravated these problems.

By assuming the role of a world policeman, the U.S. has made the goal of establishing global peace based on global cooperation more remote. Intimidation is not conducive to cooperation. In the case of the Gulf crisis, persistent diplomatic efforts coupled with non-violent frustration of the aggressor's aims (making it impossible for him to cash in on his plunder) would have restored the independence of Kuwait without destroying it and killing tens of thousands of innocent people. By participating in this war, Canada has tarnished its image as a peacekeeper. It will not be easy to restore it.

The Gulf War not only deflected huge resources which might have been used in coping with environmental degradation. It also contributed to the degradation of the environment by destroying the infrastructure of a country, by polluting the waters of the region, by instigating the destruction of oil wells. By associating itself with this orgy of destruction, Canada has damaged its reputation as a country seriously concerned with environmental protection and beginning to do something about it.

The Gulf War has aggravated the hatreds and resentments that have fueled the chronic violence in the Third World. In their desperation, the dispossessed Palestinians deluded themselves by imagining that Saddam Hussein was their champion. By voicing their support of Iraq they brought upon themselves the wrath of its enemies. The repression in the lands occupied by Israel became severely intensified. Thousands are being expelled from Kuwait. "Law and order" imposed by brute force and intimidation has always been used to oppress and torment the helpless. The following incident reported by Robert Fisk, correspondent for the Toronto Star, is revealing.

When three Kuwait soldiers began to beat up a Palestinian boy on a bicycle . . . Colin Smith of The Observer and I intervened, physically restraining the Kuwait troops and ordering them to lower their weapons . . . But the U.S. Special Forces accompanying the Kuwaitis did nothing to help.

When I asked the American officer why he allowed the Kuwaitis to beat civilians, he replied, 'You having a good day? We don't want your sort around here with your dirty rumours. You have a big mouth. This is martial law, boy. Get lost.'

In supporting the establishment of "law and order" based on force and intimidation, Canada has impaired its potential as a worker for global justice.

Opposition to U.S. hegemony will not be attenuated by a victorious blitzkrieg against a Third World country. If this opposition is centred mainly in the poor countries, it may take forms that will give the U.S. opportunities to use the mailed fist. This will not still the opposition. On the contrary, it will intensify it and raise further the level of global violence. For this reason it is important to develop centres of opposition in countries against which brute force cannot be applied so easily, nor can be as acceptable politically as punitive expeditions against Third World countries. Canada as a middle power, as a traditional friend of the American people, as an erstwhile peacekeeper (perhaps eventually rehabilitated as such) is eminently suitable as a centre of opposition to a world order based on violence and perpetual threat of violence.

NOTES

1) *Toronto Globe and Mail*, December 26, 1989.

2) *Los Angeles Times*, July 23, 1989.

3) P. Dickson, *Think Tanks*. New York: Atheneum, 1971.

4) C.J. Hitch and R.N. McKean, The Criteron Problem. In *American National Security* (M. Berkowitz and P.G. Bock, eds.) New York: The Free Press, 1965, p. 126.

5) See, for example, projected upgrading of existing search and rescue capabilities, presently administered by the National Search and Rescue Secretariat. (*News Release*, June 26, 1990). These activities could be greatly expanded if some of them were taken over by or performed in collaboration with the Department of National Defence.

6) T.R. Malthus, *An Essay on the Principle of Population*. New York: World Media Institute, 1966.

7) World Media Institute, *Tribute to Our Common Future Quarterly*, 1987/1988, p. 24.

8) The World Resource Institute, *World Resources* 1988-1989. New York: Basic Books, 1988, p. 53.

9) Ibid., p. 54.

10) Ibid., p. 114.

11) Ibid., p. 122.

12) World Media Institute, op. cit., p. 37.

13) International Development Research Centre, *The Global Research Agenda. A South-North Perspective*. Ottawa: IDRC, 1990, p. 8.

14) A recent discovery points to an unexpected source of the greenhouse effect, namely, methane, produced by termites feeding on wood. Methane is said to have 25 times the heat trapping properties of carbon dioxide. The increase in methane production has been traced to the increase of termite population – a consequence of the displacement of forests by grasslands, which termites prefer. International Development Research Centre, op. cit., pp. 13-14.

15) The World Resources Institute, op. cit., p. 135.

16) International Development Research Centre, op. cit., p. 9.

17) *World Military and Social Expenditures*, Washington: World Priorities, 1989.

18) *Toronto Star*, August 9, 1990.

19) Ibid.

20) A. Cowell, Water Rights: Plenty of Mud to Sling. *The New York Times*, February 7, 1990. Send for the Dowsers. *The Economist*, December 16, 1989, p. 42. Cited by T.F. Homer-Dixon, *Environmental Change and Violent Conflict*. International Security Studies Program Occasional Paper No. 4, Cambridge, MA, June 14, 1990.

21) P. Gleick, Climate Change and International Politics: Problems Facing Developing Countries, *Ambio*, 18, 6 (1989), pp. 333-339. Cited in T.F. Homer-Dixon, op. cit.

22) G. Porter and D. Genapin, Jr., *Resources, Population, and the Philippines' Future: A Case Study*. WRI Paper No. 4, Washington, D.C.: World Resources Institute, 1988; N. Myers, Environment and Security. *Foreign Policy*, no. 74 (1988), pp. 23-41. Cited in Homer Dixon, op. cit.

23) C. Finney and S. Western, An Economic Analysis of Environmental Protection and Management: An Example from the Philippines. *The Environmentalist*, 6, 1 (1986).

24) G. Hawes, Theories of Peasant Revolution: A Critique and Contribution from the Philippines. *World Politics*, 42, 2 (1990), pp. 261-298.

25) G. Porter and D. Ganapin, Jr., op. cit., p. 11.

26) Cf. J.S. Pustay, *Counterinsurgency Warfare*. New York: The Free Press of Glencoe 1965.

27) M. Campbell, History Shifted in a Railway Car. *Toronto Globe and Mail*, August 17, 1990.

28) E. Regehr, *Arms Canada*. Toronto: James Lorimer & Co., 1987, p. 175.

29) Ibid., p. 176.

30) Ibid.

31) Ibid., p. 177.

32) *North-South News*, Spring 1989, No. 8: Winter, 1990, No. 10.

33) S. Dale, Why Our Flourishing Arms Industry is Bad for Nation's Business, *Canada Business*, March, 1988, p. 34.

34) E. Regehr, op. cit., p. 178.

35) Ibid., p. 181-182.

36) D. Munton, Superpowers and National Security. *Peace and Security,* Winter, 1987/1988, Vol. 2, No. 4; D. Munton, Uncommon Threats and Common Security, *Peace and Security*, Winter, 1989/1990, Vol. 4, No. 4.

37) E. Regehr, op. cit., p. 185.

38) Department of External Affairs, *Competitiveness and Security* (1985), p. 14.

39) E. Regehr, op. cit., p. 186.

40) Ibid., p. xix.

41) L. Agran, *Ending the Tyranny of the Arms Race. A Peace Conversion Program.* Booklet 23 Waging Peace Series. Santa Barbara, CA: Nuclear Age Peace Foundation, 1990.

42) R. Carty and V. Smith, *Perpetuating Poverty. The Political Economy of Canada's Foreign Aid.* Toronto: Between the Lines, 1981, p. 167.

43) Ibid.

44) Ibid., p. 198.

45) Cited in Transnational Corporations: Their Global Impact. A revised version of a talk presented to Women's International League for Peace and Freedom (B.C. Branch), September 10, 1988.

46) Source: UN Centre on Transnational Corporations. *Environmental Aspects of the Activities of Transnational Corporations. A Survey.* New York: revised version of a talk presented to Women's International League for Peace and Freedom (B.C. Branch) September 10, 1988.

47) Cf. J. de Castroe. The Geopolitics of Hunger, New York: *Monthly Review Press,* 1977.

48) Cf. R. Carty and V. Smith, op. cit., Chapter 8.

49) Ibid., pp. 177-178.

50) World Media Institute, op. cit., p. 11.

51) A. Smith, *The Wealth of Nations,* New York: E.P.Dutton, Vol. 1, p. 400.

52) Ibid., p. 13.

53) George F. Kennan, Report by the Policy Planning Staff, Policy Planning Study No. 23, February 24, 1948. In *Foreign Relations of the*

United States, 1948, Volume I, Part 2. Washington: United States Government Printing Office, 1976, pp. 524-525.

54) Decisions to crush "subversion" everywhere in Europe were by no means unanimous. Britain's attitude was ambivalent, her interests having turned elsewhere – overseas, where a world empire was being built. When the Greeks revolted against their Ottoman masters, in Metternich's eyes they were a menace to the established order; but Russia wanted to help them. By 1825, the Concert of Europe was defunct.

55) D. Roche, *Building Global Security*. Toronto: NC Press, 1989, p. 19.

56) T. Hovet, *A Chronology and Fact Book of the U.N. 1941-1945*. Dells Ferry: Oceana Publications, 1986.

57) *American Journal of International Law*, Volume 80, No. 3, July, 1986. Cited by N. Singh, *The Role and Record of the International Court of Justice*. Dordrecht: Martinos Nijhoff, 1989, p. 33.

58) N. Singh, op. cit., p. 33.

59) The North-South Institute, Ottawa, Canada. *The Nervous Nineties. Review '89 Outlook '90*, p. 12.

60) G. Ernest, *Nation and Nationalism*. Oxford: Blackwell, 1983, pp. 43-50. Cited in J. Mayall, *Nationalism and International Society*, Cambridge: Cambridge University Press, 1990.

61) *Central American Report* (CAR), Guatemala, November 10, 1989; July 27; April 6; March 2, 1990; Cesar Chesala, "Central America's Health Plight," *Christian Science Monitor*, March 22, 1990; *CAR*, March 2, 1990. Cited in Noam Chomsky, "The Victors Part I," *Maga-Z-ine*, November 1990.

62) Statement made at a 35-nation seminar on military doctrine in Vienna, January 1990.

63) *Defence Industrial Preparedness. A Foundation*. Department of National Defence, 1987, p. 102. Quoted in *The Ploughshares Monitor*, September, 1988, pp. 20-21.

64) E. Regehr, op. cit., p. 195.

65) Ibid., p. 102.

66) Ibid.

67) I. Thorson, *In Pursuit of Disarmament – Conversion from Military to Civilian Production in Sweden,* Vol. 18 (From a conversion study commissioned by the Swedish government).

68) E. Regehr, op. cit., p. 216.

69) E. Regehr, Canada Targets the Third World. *This Magazine,* February 1, 1987.

70) Ibid. and *Arms Canada.* Chapter 1. See also Chapter IV above on wars involving Third World countries.

71) E. Kepp, Booming Business: Arms Sales. *The Ploughshares Monitor,* September, 1988, p. 22.

72) More specific information about conversion preparations may be found in Seymour Melman, *The Demilitarized Society: Disarmament and Conversion.* Montreal: Harvest House, 1988; also in Project Ploughshares Canada working paper, *Peace, Employment, and the Economics of Permanent War,* 1984.

73) E. Regehr, *Arms Canada,* p. 215.

74) The Right Honourable Joe Clark, Minister of External Affairs. Speech at the United Nations International Conference on the Relationship of Disarmament and Development. (New York, August 24, 1987), p. 1.

75) U. Franklin, Let's Put Science under the Microscope. *Toronto Globe and Mail,* August 28, 1990.

76) T.G. Weiss, Leading the Horse to Water, *Peace and Security,* V, 1 (Spring, 1990), p. 8.

Achevé   Imprimerie
d'imprimer Gagné Ltée
au Canada Louiseville

9 780888 666369